She

is

Magic

*A Magical Collaboration of
17 Women Sharing their Magic
with the World*

*She is Magic Book Series
Blair Hayse Publishing
a Division of Blair Hayse,
International, LLC*

First Edition

Copyright 2020 © Blair Hayse Publishing

www.blairhayse.com

All Rights Reserved

ISBN: 9798634658131

No part of this book may be reproduced or transmitted in any form or by any means, electronical or mechanical, including photocopying, recording or by an information storage and retrieval system – except by a reviewer who may quote brief passages in a review to be printed in a magazine, newspaper or on the Web – without permission in writing from the publisher.

Cover Design by: Mystic Design – Branding & Web
http://www.franmatteini.com

This book is dedicated to all those who have magic inside them and use it to profoundly impact the world around them. I truly believe that every person has magic in them, whether they have realized it or not. I encourage you to dig deep and find that magic. Use it to spread hope to the world around you and sprinkle it wherever you may go.

So, do not be fooled, I promise,

there is magic within each of you.

Enjoy the magic...

Table of Contents

- xi   *Introduction*
  Blair Hayse

- 1   *Pause, Reflect, Inspire*
  Jennifer Kirch

- 14   *Finding My Way Back*
  Rachel Peulen

- 26   *The Secret is Out*
  Heather Scott

- 36   *Stronger than the Falls*
  Kim Yoos

- 49   *Carry my Books and Walk Along Beside Me, Please*
  Linda O. Carducci

- 61   *Out of the Darkness*
  Amanda Kijek

- 72   *Just A Girl Who Decided to Go for It*
  Gretel Leach

- 84   *Girl, Don't Fall on Your Face*
  Emily Blake

95 *From Victim to Victor*
    Kim Pierre

107 *Blazing my Own Trail*
    Dawn Broadwater

117 *Standing in Truth and Walking in Balance*
    Alicia Thorp

126 *Finding Serendipity*
    Anne Marie Moorer

137 *Magic of Flight*
    Molly Peebles

147 *My Two Seasons*
    Janet Brent

159 *A Life Full of Memories*
    Millie Kate Denhof

168 *Go Ahead and Jump*
    Eleni ELNRG

179 *Nice Girls Don't Get the Plush Corner Office (Or Do They?)*
    Blair Hayse

Introduction

Blair Hayse

When I had the vision of the *She is Magic* book series, it came from a place of women being able to share their own personal story of magic. I wanted them to use their stories to help themselves heal, to inspire others, to give others hope and to reach an exciting goal they each had to become a published author. I believe each of us holds an element of magic in our own unique story. A story that could have caused us to throw in the towel and quit, but instead we found what we were really made of and held on. We chose to reach out to a higher being and trust that all things happen *for* us instead of *to* us.

I have always loved to write and had the privilege of having parents who encouraged me as a young girl to write whenever I could. They helped me form books and learn as much as I can. I applied for a writing college and was accepted when I was young adult. It should not have surprised me as many people told me I was a talented writer, but it still shocked me that I was accepted. I pursued getting an education in writing children's books and adult books. Whenever I could, I chose to write. I was published in several places both in print and digitally through the years. It was a completely no brainer decision for me to decide to put together a series for women to collaborate and become authors on a journey together. I knew I wanted the experience to be one that was fun, full of excitement and the ability to learn the publishing process so that they could repeat this process on their own if they ever wanted. I wanted to help them understand the beauty of writing and sharing their story. I wanted them to feel supported through the whole process. As I began to work on this project my love for writing and helping others flowed through every aspect of it.

When I put this idea out there for the first book in the series, I was amazed at the outstanding response from women who resonated with the title and message for the book. Women who had an amazing story to tell of their magic. I cannot tell you the messages I got from women who just knew it was meant for them by the title. So much of a response that we went over our 15-author cap we had placed on the co-author spots when we were preparing the book. The book ended up being filled with 17 stories of magical women who will inspire you as you turn the pages. This book is extra special to me because my daughter is also a co-author in this book. This is the first book we have been co-authors in and I hope there are many more to follow. As my team began to put together the book and help the authors construct their chapters the responses of women interested in collaborating with the book kept flooding in. We ended up having to put together a wait list for those who were interested in being a part of another book. It was immediately seen that this would be a series and that more *She is Magic* books were in our near future.

So much of our media and surroundings are filled with negative news it can become heavy at times. People crave being able to hear the stories of those who overcame. Those who were able to rise from the ashes and create a new life. Do not worry. That is what this book delivers in every way possible.

I want to say a thank you to all the women who filled this book because I know how brave and vulnerable you had to be in order to share these stories. I am so proud of each of you for stepping into the gap and using your stories to help others. I want to say thank you to my graphic designer Fran who created a beautiful cover for the book that perfectly represents me, my brand and the message this book conveys. I want to say thank you to my assistant Olivia for all her hard work in helping me put this book together and getting it ready to submit for publishing. Thank you to Janet for her hard work in helping the book be formatted correctly and loaded in under all the right places. I am forever grateful to my parents David and Teresa who encouraged me to write from as a child and even as an adult. They have always been my biggest inspirations. Thank you to my husband Jeremy who stands beside me and cheers me on during all my projects I take on. Thank you to my children Parker, Millie and Jackson who are the sunshine of my life. Special thank you to Millie for continuing to choose to pursue her writing passions even in this book with her chapter. May you continue to do what lights up your soul. Thank you to all my former bosses and co-workers who have given me the inspiration for my chapter in this book. I could not be the success in business I am today without all of you who touched my life in such amazing ways.

If you are looking for something to read that is going to make you cry and laugh at the same time because it is so raw…then this book is for you. You will literally feel the emotions intertwined through these stories as you read them. These women held nothing back as they shared with you some of their innermost struggles, points of healing, lowest points and highest accomplishments. They are authentic throughout their stories. They take you on the journey with them and you will not want to put it down as you begin to read.

As you read be aware of your own stories found inside of you. Be aware of how sharing that story can inspire others and give others hope. It is more than just a "story."

It is a journey of victory. It is a story of magic that you can sprinkle wherever you choose to go. Leave others with hope and inspiration just by being you. Never... I repeat... NEVER... hide your magic.

In summary this book...

It is filled with hope.
It is filled with inspiration.
It is filled with love.
It is filled with healing.
It is filled with stories of women who rise up.
It is filled with lots of magic.

Enjoy and know that this book is filled with lots of love just for you.

Pause, Reflect, Inspire

Jennifer Kirch

I always enjoyed being a giver. Never one for conflict, having the ability to be of service to friends and family has made me feel fantastic even from a young age. A friend's mother continually said as I was growing up, that my hobby was helping others.

It's no surprise that many of my dating relationships weren't super successful because of putting more energy into others than myself. Hitting rock bottom and going through a painful divorce was when I learned how to truly love and value myself.

At that time, I was introduced to yoga which was certainly the wakeup call I needed. Healthy for both body and mind, and there was something I absolutely loved about the community. So much of my life was based on others, especially as a school teacher, and it completely depleted me. Finally, I was doing something nurturing for me.

The teachings in yoga and meditation classes were life-changing. One message that resonated the most was, "You can't pour from an empty cup."

Although not the strongest yogi, I was ultra-dedicated signing up for as many workshops, trainings, retreats, and soaking in all knowledge possible. My resume now includes certified yoga teacher, kid's yoga teacher, Trauma Informed Yoga Teacher, Divine Sleep® Yoga Nidra teacher, certified Reiki Level 1, practitioner of Mindfulness Based Stress Reduction, The Seven Attitudinal Foundations of Mindfulness, ISHTA Trained Meditation Teacher, and currently working on my Socio-Emotional Learning certification.

The majority of this work came before diagnosed with stage 4 metastatic breast cancer on Mother's Day of 2018. These tools have been invaluable, and I truly believe that I am here today because of these practices. I have always identified with being an empathetic person, but these past almost two years have given me a whole new appreciation of the many beautiful souls living with, during, and beyond a cancer diagnosis.

The things you go through and grow through on a daily basis forever change your perspective... priorities... goals... battles... milestones... friendships... fears... This dis-ease has completely changed every aspect of my life and continues to take from me physically... emotionally...

financially... I don't see anything through the same eyes since my diagnosis.

Nothing is taken for granted, and miracles are seen daily. Things that I once thought would be nightmares, have come and gone. I've survived – and it's only served to make me stronger. I've seen and felt more love in these past two years than most people feel in their entire lifetime. For that, I am abundantly grateful.

I can't even imagine how this has affected my family. My mother is a three-time survivor. Luckily, she has never had to go through the kinds of treatments as I have. My sister is several states away, and only so much can get translated through phone calls, texts, and some visits which I know causes tremendous worry and stress. My father has been my rock and emotional support throughout this journey. He's seen the good, the bad and the downright scary. All the while, with his quiet strength and calm demeanor has helped me see the good in so many situations that could have gone either way. His endless patience with driving me to countless medical appointments, being the voice of reason, and simply being himself. I would never want to go through any of this again, but the silver lining is that we've never had the amount of time together as we do now, and have bonded in a way we never would have without this dis-ease. We didn't always have this relationship, and for this, I am forever indebted.

Making the best of my situation was my priority. I never once asked why this happened to me and promised myself not to go down the rabbit hole of looking up information about stage 4 metastatic breast cancer on the internet. The best part of this challenge was that it has taken me through so many aspects of my life and even with everything going on medically, I am filled with gratitude daily.

It's easy to get wrapped up with the negatives of this dis-ease. However, since my journey began, I have realized I have an army of support like no other. What a blessing it is to hear daily from people from every area of my life: elementary school through graduate school friends, teaching colleagues, former students, former teachers, waitressing friends, girl scout camp friends, the yoga/mindfulness/meditation community, family members, former roommates, fun friends I've met along the way, former neighbors, sorority sisters, new friends... you name it, people from my entire lifetime have shown extreme love and compassion. To each of you, please look in the mirror and know that I see you, I appreciate you, and I am so grateful. From the bottom of my heart, thank you for lifting me up, being a part of the healing process, and mostly for making me feel so incredibly loved. I don't take any of this for granted.

At the same time, not everyone is able to handle being a part of this journey. Although many friends have stepped up tremendously, some friends have completely stepped out. I could lie and say that this doesn't hurt, but I have come to understand that cancer affects people differently. One of the most challenging lessons to learn is that some people that you counted on and cared about for years, either don't know what to say, or simply no longer choose to be a part of your life with this dis-ease.

Although usually a private person, I have been documenting my journey through social media which included numerous humbling events – my mother being diagnosed at the same time, losing my home, car, ability to work, long red hair, and even my body as I knew it. When originally asked why I was open to sharing such personal information, I answered that people wouldn't be able to pray for me if they didn't know.

I went out on my first leave in May of 2018. The vice on my head that I had mistaken for the longest, most intense migraine ever, was actually a lesion in my skull. My first treatment was radiation to my skull. Locked down to the table strapped in by a helmet, I spent the entire process meditating and visualizing perfect health.

My "high maintenance" requests to the radiation team were simply a warm blanket and Zen music. Apparently, this impacted one of the technicians greatly. Noticing my calmness, he stated that because of our interaction, listening to Zen music instead of the news is how he now begins his day on a positive note.

Since I'm a firm believer that life tends to give you exactly what you need. No matter what, I always expressed gratitude and was thankful. Each experience provided me with a new lesson to learn.

Since my diagnosis, I depleted twenty-four years of sick leave. It was beyond humbling to have to apply for grants, have benefits held so that I could pay for my medical benefits, and a Go Fund Me page in order to keep paying bills.

An extremely good friend that I have known since I was two years old, helped me to advocate to my doctors, and that I needed a plan medically that would allow me to get back to school in September to keep both my job and medical benefits. This meant that my entire summer was three back to back intensive surgeries.

One of the medications that they gave me for a year and a half during chemotherapy was supposed to strengthen my bones. Instead, it caused a portion of my jawbone to die and I needed surgery to have it extracted as well as a tooth that cracked from the inside.

Everything I identified as a woman, has been challenged by this disease: my chest, my hair, my smile. I have truly had to put the yogic philosophy of "I am not my body" into place every time I look into a mirror.

As of writing this, I have had twenty-eight office visits to the oncologist, seven office visits to the radiologist, three office visits to the oncology surgeon, nine office visits to the plastic surgeon, nine additional doctor/specialist visits, seven hospital admissions, five surgeries – two either cancelled or changed while waiting in the operating room, eighteen days in the hospital, thirty-eight chemotherapy treatments in addition to taking oral chemotherapy daily, eight visits to the oral surgeon, fifty radiation treatments, nine various body scans, and endless prescriptions and supplements. My body feels butchered and there are scars everywhere.

It proved that life gives you the tools to handle, you just need to be receptive and open. God is going to give you what you can manage. These experiences raised my gratitude and opened my eyes to the toxicity in my previous life. It helped enlighten me and remove what was no longer serving me.

Over this lifetime, I've woven together the most beautiful tapestry of amazing people. The amount of love and support pouring out through family and friends from every area of my life is like no other! No matter what was happening with my physical body, I was surrounded in more love than anyone could ever imagine.

People constantly mention how strong I am, but it isn't always what I think of strength. It comes in all forms:

learning to speak up, learning to say no, learning to ask for help when you've been independent your whole life, sometimes just getting out of bed, smiling through the pain, being grateful for those who choose to stand by you, trying to understand why others have distanced themselves and working on not taking it so personally, being open to all forms of healing, learning a "new normal," accepting change, keeping out fear, the power of prayer, the power of love, the power of gratitude, listening to your body, eating even when it's no longer enjoyable, accepting that this dis-ease takes away choices, so much more than I can list.

The "new normal" includes dealing with chronic pain daily, taking medications that leave you mentally and physically exhausted – as well as interfering with your appetite, and self-pressure knowing what you used to be able to do. Adding to that insurance company's decisions that you can only have a certain amount of migraines per month or denying life-saving scans or medications. This constant battle is absolutely exhausting.

A wonderful friend mentioned in our telephone call one day that, "even warriors get weary." Words can't express my gratitude when I found an incredibly special gift in my mailbox when I got home: a specially designed sweatshirt that reads: "Rise Up. Battle On." Oh, how I wear that with pride.

This journey has offered the opportunity to help others who are either newly diagnosed, in recovery, or living with cancer. A series of events led me to be a guest blogger offering candid details about how this dis-ease changes you physically. I truly did not realize just drastically my physical appearance altered in one short year.

As raw of an experience as that was, I realized that I could share my knowledge with other cancer survivors and thrivers. Always loving fashion, I have been able to share outfit recommendations for what to wear after various medical procedures or to hide medical equipment. My idea of creating a blog to help others came to life then.

When possible, offering pop up Yoga Nidra healings at different studios and day spas brings me inexplicable joy. In meditation offerings, I frequently guide others to visualize a golden light of healing as that is what I see when meditating.

Interestingly enough, a friend asked me for my Jewish name so she could pray for me at her synagogue. For years, I thought my name translated to "Beautiful Flower" – but apparently that was my sister's name. Mine, Zahavah Meirah, translates to "Golden Light." This reassures me that I am aligned with my life's purpose.

The best part of this challenge was that it has taken me through so many aspects of my life and even with everything going on medically, I am filled with gratitude daily. It's easy to get wrapped up with the negatives of this dis-ease. However, since my journey began, I have realized I have a supportive army like no other.

There are miracles daily... and I am so grateful for the ability that when we pause, we are able to see them more often and more clearly.

It's not a club that you ever want to join, but you can make the best of it. I'm grateful for all the yoga, trauma, mindfulness, and meditation training that prepared me leading up to this. I can only imagine how differently these past two years would have played out differently without these tools.

I don't have to know how, but I have faith that everything will work out, and that this will be both a blessing and a lesson. Miracles happen every day. We just need time to pause and reflect on them.

Lesson upon lesson has come to me, and I constantly learn: be present, be humble, be grateful. "Gratitude is the ultimate state of receivership," Dr. Joe Dispenza.

Multiple times, I thought I was completely overwhelmed and broken, but never in my life have I been surrounded by so much love and support. What amazed me was where this came from. People truly went above and beyond. I'm grateful for the incredible support system I've had since my diagnosis.

Yoga and mindfulness lessons have become all too real – learning to appreciate the little things, I am not my body, and how mindset changes everything. "Your strength is how calmly, quietly, and peacefully you face life," Yogi Bhajan.

ABOUT JENNIFER KIRCH

Jennifer grew up outside of Ocean City, NJ. She attended The College of New Jersey, formerly known as Trenton State College, for both undergraduate and graduate studies. She received her BA in Sociology and Psychology in 1992 and her Masters of Arts in Teaching in 1994.

Upon graduation, the lure of living at the beach brought her back home. She's been a public-school teacher since 1994 teaching all subjects in elementary school and currently teaching 6th Grade Middle School English.

Jennifer loves her community and proudly supports small businesses. She enjoys fashion, learning, reading, travel, yoga, mindfulness and meditation.

A certified yoga and meditation teacher, she thrives on learning more about mindfulness, meditation, numerous healing modalities, and how to bring socio-emotional wellness to others.

Diagnosed with stage 4 metastatic breast cancer in May of 2018, Jennifer has inspired many with her healing journey. She is blessed beyond words and forever grateful for her family and friends who have created an army of support and love like no other.

Jennifer is the founder of Pause and Reflect Yoga, LLC, and The Warrior's Voice Blog.

She shares her home with the beautiful Kwan Yin, a Maine Coon rescue who is extremely outgoing, lovable, and healing beyond belief. Luckily, this feline lives up to her namesake – the goddess of loving kindness, compassion. And healing.

To connect with Jennifer:
Facebook: Pause and Reflect Yoga
Instagram: jmk_pause
Website: pauseandreflectyoga.com
Email: pause.and.reflect.yoga@gmail.com

Finding My Way Back

Rachel Peulen

If you have ever been through something traumatic and struggled to see a light at the end of the tunnel, you are not alone.

Imagine starting the day off the same way as usual. You get dressed, have your morning coffee, drive to work and everything falls in line with your daily routine. This has been me many times (minus the coffee), but I'm not here to talk to you about routines. Instead, I'm here to share a traumatic event that has changed my life.

Take a moment to picture this... I'm at work which for me is a Special Education administrator at a school. I am making my rounds and checking on my team. I greet students and the day begins like all normal days before. However, not long into the day, I am called to help with a crisis situation. As I arrive in the classroom that has already been evacuated; I find papers creating a blanketed white cover over the classroom carpet and desks with chairs tipped completely over. I walk to the back of the room where I can distinctly detect banging in the closet. I notice the closet door is being unlocked. I am greeted by the assistant principal and the student's case manager. As the closet door opens, the student has put a hole in a wall and is working hard to break a bookshelf inside. Destruction of property is one thing and can be fixed or replaced, so we let him direct his rage at maiming the bookshelf. However, it did not take long for the situation to take a turn in a direction where the student had put his own safety at risk. At this point, I knew I had to go from being an observer to taking action; in order to keep this boy safe from his own unraveling. Keep in mind, this boy was about the same height as me. I attempted to escort him out of the closet and that's when it happened. One blow from the back of his head…to the front of my face. A headbutt with such force that it led to a ricochet effect where my head was hoisted backwards and the back of my head hit the wall. Fast forward through a rigorous amount of what many people who have been in car accidents call whiplash, defined as an injury caused by a severe jerk to the head. This continuous whiplash lasted for over 30 minutes. Then, there was a second head butt, this one causing the same ricochet effect, only this time, the back of my head hit a cement wall.

Intense. The entire situation was intense. From monitoring the vicious cycle of self-destruction for this boy; knowing his wheels were turning, knowledge that his head was filled with many thoughts and feelings, such as: frustration, confusion and added with an inability to process everything necessary for his mind to make sense of it all prior to turning to a mode of destruction. Ultimately, a call to action was required until this boy was able to show within the confines of his troubled spirit that he was regaining control and could be safely released from the limits pressed upon him by his own undoing. He had self-destructed that day and had left that destruction in his wake. Destruction in ways that he would never be able to comprehend. Unfortunately, I was a casualty of his own demise. Although I did not know it at the time, my life was about to forever change. I'm not talking about a little change here either; I'm talking about the kind of change that has led me to where I am today; over two years later.

That day, I received a Traumatic Brain Injury. Interestingly enough, doctors told me to keep working. In a time when I thought a person who receives a brain injury should take time to rest; times had changed. The first signs of this disability were sensitivity to light, loud noises and terrible headaches. I had never had many headaches in my life prior to this incident. It didn't take long for these headaches to become debilitating; causing me to miss an average of two days of work per week. My neurologist had me in physical therapy, occupational therapy and speech therapy twice a week for each modality of therapy. I continued to work and very quickly started noticing large discrepancies in my ability to speak fluently. I was frequently losing words mid-sentence and even losing an entire train of thought. Part of my job as an administrator is to attend all due process meetings for the building that I work in. In these particular meetings, I do a lot of talking and I found it to be quite embarrassing to not be able to speak or recall what I wanted to say anymore. If I was the notetaker (a job I had to delegate to others pretty quickly after the crisis, due to the computer screen time being too much for me and I was learning to pick my battles), I could not keep track of what a person was saying long enough to get it all typed. I would temporarily have to stop the meeting to ask for the person to repeat part of what they were saying or ask clarifying questions. When I was leading a meeting, I would easily lose what I was trying to say or lose the ability to identify the word I wanted. This created impatience among my staff members. They tried hard to work with me and to be patient, but I know that it was hard for them at times. It was hard for me too. In fact, it was infuriating. This was not me. This was not my normal. I was a fluent and composed speaker, not whatever this was. I was a person who went from being a multi-tasker and having a strong memory to needing to have a calendar laid out with every little thing I needed to do placed on it. I had lost my organizational capabilities. I couldn't remember things people would tell me, which was not only frustrating for me, but was also very frustrating for those I worked with. I found that I could no longer balance all of my job duties, as I had been able to do prior to this crisis.

As time progressed for the next five months following the injury; what were once my strengths, were now daily challenges that affected my ability to perform my job. At first, the school staff, especially my fellow leadership members and the special education team I managed, were very understanding and patient. However, with any injury that is invisible, it is hard to understand what all it encompasses or the depth and brevity with which one's life is affected unless it has happened to you. Since the injury was invisible, people expected me to bounce right back and could not understand why I was struggling with things as simple as remembering what someone had said from one minute to the next. Needless to say, the period of understanding or what I call a grace period was very short lived and expectations were high that I could perform my job the way in which it was intended to be performed. Did I need to cut my hours? It was something my speech therapist was concerned about. She would talk to me about how I might be able to balance a work week if I cut my hours in half. I shared with her my fear of being an overachiever, knowing that I would attempt to complete all of my work in the shortened day and it would ultimately make my symptoms worse. In the end, I had my neurology team write up a letter. It stated that of the school day hours, I would work half of those hours from home and would spend the other half resting my head or going to appointments.

I was put on medical leave. Per what the letter stated, I was unable to perform my job duties according to the principal, who told me that my job was more socially based than home based. I would not be able to observe the staff I supervised or coach them. I would not be able to work with students in any capacity anymore. This was a very difficult time for me. I had not expected medical leave as an outcome to the letter. This became a very dark time for me. I spent my days alone. I did not want to get out of bed. I could not really do anything even if I did get out of bed. Occasionally if I could stay up long enough without a migraine, I could help get my children ready for school. This was a major feat, that rarely happened. The only thing I could really do was listen to books on my kindle and even that, I did in bed. I became depressed and would only leave the house if I had a neurology appointment. Those were every six weeks. I had taken a break from my other therapies. Since I was resting my brain from work; I was also resting it from therapy. Emotionally, mentally and physically I was exhausted. I thought everything that had happened leading up to medical leave was my fault. I fell into a pattern of self-doubt and self-sabotage. I had also become very anxious. I was afraid to have my children home with me alone. My emotions had gone astray so much; that if someone dropped a pin I would cry. I had lost control of who I was and of all I had been capable of. I could see no light in the tunnel I was traveling through. The darkness is powerful. It tends to strip you down to your rawest and most vulnerable state. For well over six months, every day I wished to turn back time, starting with not having gone to work that day. I didn't want anyone else to have to deal with what I was, but I did want my life back. I wanted to be myself again, not someone who had this disability where I could not speak correctly, could not remember anything and cognitively could not process things.

This has not only been a challenging time for me, but also a challenging time for my family. My husband has always done his best to support me. He read what he could about supporting someone who has a brain injury. Although he feels at a loss to support much of the time, for me…he has been my rock! He tries to listen to me and wait when I am trying to say something, but cannot find the words. Things that seem so simple to remember the name of, such as a dishwasher, I often cannot recall. My husband has been so patient with me through this entire journey and has definitely been doing everything in his power to help me and take care of our children when I am unable to do so. I truly do not know where I would be without him by my side, supporting me, loving me, listening to me and holding me when life becomes too much. My children have also been affected by this brain injury. They do not understand what I am going through and think I should be all better. It is hard for them to empathize with me when I am unable to play with them because of a migraine. They cannot comprehend the stages I have been going through. For them, the reality of this invisible injury really hits the mark and with this lack of understanding, their words can sting at times. However, they are present and they love me. They want me to be happy and healthy. My parents have been very supportive! It hurts them deeply to see all I have been going through, but they are always there for me. My mom has offered to come over to help clean, play with the kids, paint and so much more. Without my parents, I probably would have never stepped out of the house. They started coming over consistently to help me get outside and help me in the yard while my husband was still at work. It is crazy, but I truly believe my mom has more energy now than I ever will.

Over the years, I have learned so much. The why behind my Traumatic Brain Injury is still unfolding before me. For the longest time I could not see a light in the tunnel of my life. Now I see the light and it is guiding me as I continue to heal. Even with the triumphs and setbacks, I am no longer allowing this disability to control me. I am not the same person I was prior to being injured. It may sound odd, but I literally had to mourn the death of my old self, a self I loved, so I could be reborn like that of a Phoenix rising from the ashes of its former self. I am a work in progress, trying to figure out who this person I am still getting to know is. I have taken the time to dig deeply from within, to positively rebuild and become realigned on my own journey of self-discovery. I have not gone back into the field of education; as my executive functioning skills are still limited. However, I have started working in the online space and I now help people on their journey of self-discovery. Everyone is capable of so much and having a strong internal belief system is important. It is when our internal self is strong that we can bring it to the outside and let it shine... that's where the magic happens!

ABOUT RACHEL PEULEN

Rachel Peulen was born and raised in Lake Elmo, Minnesota. After graduating high school in 1999, she attended Minnesota State University Moorhead, receiving her bachelor's degree in Special Education. Rachel taught Special Education to children with severe to profound disabilities for 15 years. During this time, she earned her Master's in Education and later went on to receive her K-12 Principal and Director of Special Education licenses. After 15 years of teaching, Rachel became a Special Education Administrator.

When not teaching and helping others, Rachel embraces time with her family. She also enjoys reading, warm summer days, game nights and lunch dates with her mother. Rachel currently resides in Hudson, WI with her husband Matthew and their two beautiful children, Hailey and Violet.

Although Rachel is no longer working in the field of education; she has moved into the online space where she still works to help people on a daily basis. She is a digital marketing strategist and a personal development coach. She shows women who are ready to leave their 9-5 corporate job a way to take action to become successful online entrepreneurs.

Rachel's superpower is to guide women on a journey of self-discovery. She does this by digging deeply with them to strengthen their inner self so their outer self can reflect that strength and in turn, creates space for self-belief, alignment and success.

Rachel is an author and speaker, as well as the owner of RGP Innovative Marketing, LLC. She has founded a Facebook group, *"Affiliate Marketing Success Seekers,"* for those women who are ready to leave their 9-5 corporate job to become a successful online entrepreneur. Rachel also offers free resources: a Take Action, Reach Your Goals action plan, a Social Media Content Calendar, a 5-day free Learn the Untapped Opportunities of Affiliate Marketing challenge, and a YouTube channel. She also runs a Release Your 9-5 Job six-month training and coaching program.

You can connect with Rachel here:

Facebook business page:
www.facebook.com/strengthenconnections

Instagram:
www.instagram/rachelpeulen

Website:
www.rachelpeulen.com

The Secret is Out

Heather Scott

You could easily say, life has not been easy for me. I grew up on a tiny island, Fogo Island, off the coast of Newfoundland, as far east as you can go before hitting Greenland. It is an island accessible only by a boat or helicopter. I was born in the mid-eighties, an only child to Kirk and Esther, and somewhat of a difficult child, or so I have been told. When I was three years old, my parents noticed a tiny bald spot in my long beautiful blonde hair. All of this unbeknown to me, my hair grew back in and I went on to live a normal childhood up until I reached the 5th grade.

One day I was sitting in my 5th grade class and a classmate pointed out to me that there was a huge patch of hair missing on the right side of my head. That morning, before school, my dad put my hair up. He had placed it half up and half down; just how I liked to wear it. Surely it was not like that when I left the house this morning? I don't think it was at least? It's like out of nowhere my hair just literally fell out in one giant chunk. I still wonder, to this day, if the janitor of the school ever found a bunch of hair?! I had no idea what was going on with me. I ran to the bathroom to see this for myself and sure enough my hair was gone on that one side. I immediately darted down to the principal's office hysterical. They allowed me to leave school and go to my mom's work just across the street. I scampered to my mom crying and she had this look on her face, as if she knew exactly what it was. I was so scared. I thought I was dying.

After going off of the island to visit a dermatologist; it was confirmed that I had alopecia areata. Never heard of alopecia areata? Me neither! Apparently, it is an autoimmune disorder that causes unpredictable hair loss. It actually affects about 6.8 million people in the United States. Usually the hair falls out in small patches. It can lead to the complete loss of hair on the scalp (alopecia totalis) or, in other cases, the entire body (alopecia universalis). The condition can affect anyone, regardless of age and gender, though most cases occur before the age of 30.

So here I am, eight years old and my hair is falling out like crazy. I'm trying steroid creams to stimulate hair growth on my scalp, getting hundreds of steroid injections all over my scalp where the hair has fallen out and screaming in pain combined with fear and just wanting it all to be over with. This trauma went on for several years. I did not lose all my hair, but I came close to it. I had the craziest short haircut the following year. I hated to look at myself in the mirror. Kids would tease me and call me "baldy". I had friends, but life was not easy as a kid and especially merged with me losing my hair. I remember a few boys sticking up for me when others were bullying me. I will never forget their kindness on the playground. As a child, I never wanted to hear talk of a wig. I just wanted to be normal again and have my hair back.

When 7th grade rolled around, near Halloween of that year, I was still battling my hair loss. I suddenly started to become super thirsty all the time. I craved juice! I would wake up in the middle of the night and I would drink a whole jug of juice. My mom took me to the small cottage hospital on the island and before we left that day it was confirmed I had type 1 diabetes. I was SO scared. All I knew was that there was another boy in my class named Brian; who was also a type 1 diabetic. I knew that I was going to have to give myself needles like he did. I was told that day I could go home for Halloween, but not to eat any sugar. I would then have to spend two weeks in a hospital, off the island, to learn how to treat myself with insulin. At this point I hated everything about my life. My hair was falling out and I had to give myself needles just to stay alive. I cried and refused to take my needles. I gave my parents the hardest time of their life. I remember my mom trying to give me my insulin in my arm and I would pull away causing her to scrape my arm with the syringe. Life was so tough and honestly, I hated it. I hated the diabetes. I hated the alopecia. Why me?! How could God be so cruel?? I would pray every night to God. I would thank Him for everything in my life, but I would also ask Him to stop my hair from falling out or not to fall out any more than it already had.

My parents didn't have medical insurance and diabetic supplies were very expensive. My grandma, my aunt and my uncle lived north of Toronto. They were able to get my dad a job there that had medical benefits. Not too long after being diagnosed with diabetes, we moved from this tiny remote island with the population of only a few thousand, to a large city. I was super anxious about the move. I had to meet new friends. I was 12 years old. I looked funny because of my hair. I talked funny, because you all know what a newfie accent sounds like. I still had to give myself needles and I did not want to tell anyone. I kept it all inside. I felt anxious all the time. I would throw up every day before school. I met a girl named Andrea, who had just moved to Canada and hardly spoke English; as Hungarian was her native language. She was my first friend I made in the new city and I held onto her tightly. She is my best friend still to this day!

After that, life got a little better. My hair seemed to start growing back in enough that I could cover my hair loss. I went to high school and things were looking good. I played rugby and field hockey. I found that playing tough sports gave me the confidence that nobody would mess with me.

I still never told people about my alopecia. It was no one's business. My mom and I would get creative by sewing hair extensions into headbands that I could wear to school or wear while I played sports to give me some extra coverage. When 10th grade rolled around, my hair started rapidly falling out again. I got away with hair extensions for a while, but this time it was so bad I needed to get a wig. I HATED the thought of wearing a wig. I felt like everyone would know it was a wig, but I had no choice at this point. I could NOT go to school with a bald head...I just couldn't. Highschool is hard enough as it is, let alone going to high school without hair! I survived wearing a wig. I would try to wear headbands and other accessories in efforts to make it look less obvious. Thankfully, I think it worked! I never told anyone my secret, not even my best friend in high school.

After high school, I went on to attend college. I attended college to become a police officer. Despite my parents telling me no, I chose to do it anyways. It was in college that I met my husband. We never dated in college, but we went there together and took the same classes. Ironically enough, neither of us ever became police officers. I never had any problems dating, but I also did not tell anyone I dated about my hair loss. I had a rule that they were never to touch my hair! After college, I started working for a large corporate company. I worked my way up in the company and spent the last 15 years of my career there. During those 15 years, I started dating my now husband (yes, the one from college). It took me dating him a long time before I told him about my hair loss. I was sick to my stomach with nerves telling him. He was totally supportive and always loved me for who I am. We got married and had three amazing children. We traveled the world together. I never let my hair loss get in the way of me living my best life. I could swim, play sports, work out…all while wearing a wig!

In 2019, while being on maternity leave with my daughter, I had this calling inside me. I felt the need to help others with their hair loss. I am not sure exactly how it happened, but one day I decided I'm going to open an online wig boutique to help other women and children like myself. The only problem? I didn't want to tell anyone about my hair loss! What would my co-workers think? I had worked there for 15 years and no one knew I wore a wig. My best friend from high school? She did not know that I wore a wig and I was going to be her maid of honor. I felt like a fake or fraud. I felt as if I had been living this double life for nearly 30 years. I was hiding from my hair loss, under my wig. So, after 30 years of trying everything possible to hide my hair loss, I came out on social media. Posting a side by side photo of my bald head and the other of me rocking a gorgeous wig. People were SHOCKED! But you know what? I had to do it. If I wanted to help others, I needed them to be able to find me. I had this instant relief! All the weight I had been carrying for so many years, was now lifted off my shoulders. My secret was out! This is me; this is the real Heather and damn I am so proud of her!!

In 2020 I launched my online wig business: *Pretty Wigs to You*. People were instantly drawn to me in the hair loss community. I am relatable because I keep it real. I post pictures of me rocking amazing Jon Renau wigs and I post pictures of my bald head. I never thought I would be helping so many women and children feel more confident about wearing a wig. Every day I get to wake up and know I am genuinely helping people. It is such a rewarding feeling. My first priority is to help others! I have dealt with alopecia for 30 years. I am definitely an expert in this field. People reach out to me at their first hair loss experience. They are scared. They are worried. They want their hair to grow back. I am there for them just like I was for that scared little girl I was in my past. I answer people's questions and concerns. I give them resources and advice. I am their friend when they need one. My business comes second to the relationship I form with them. I help women in need even when they cannot afford a wig. I help children going through hair loss and I provide them resources for free wigs. If there are no resources in their area; I purchase the wig for them and send it to them for free. Children hold a special place in my heart. Childhood is hard enough; despite it being coupled with going through hair loss or childhood cancer. That is devastating to a child and if I can help boost their confidence, even a little, then my work is done!

I do not want people to feel bad for me. I turned my life around, maybe it was by my constant prayers each and every night. I stopped the "poor me" attitude and I decided to quit the pity party. I decided to take charge of my own life. I could have easily fell into a depression about my hair, my diabetes or my looks. Instead, I realized once I stopped complaining about my life, it got a whole lot better. Counting my blessings has really opened me up to living my best life each day. I have an amazingly supportive husband; three wonderfully healthy children and I was brave enough to open myself up to the world with my deepest dark secret. In doing this, I have been able to help so many women and children along the way! I am truly blessed in my life. Always remember, the universe has bigger plans for all of us! It may not make any sense at the time things happen, but if you put your trust in God and the universe... you can do so many amazing magical things!

ABOUT HEATHER SCOTT

Heather Scott is the owner of Pretty Wigs to You, an online wig boutique specializing in medical grade wigs and toppers for women going through hair loss. Heather is an alopecia wig expert. She loves helping others feel beautiful and confident about wearing a wig.

Heather has had alopecia since the age of three, so children with hair loss hold a soft spot in her heart. Heather often provides free resources and wigs to the children due to this. She has spent a lifetime of covering up her own hair loss and has since had a calling to help others like herself. She has recently come out to the world about her hair loss.

Heather lives in Toronto Canada with her husband and three kids. She enjoys being a hockey mom, traveling the world with her family, and running her successful business.

How to Connect with Heather:

Website:
www.prettywigstoyou.com
www.helperhairbox.com

Social Media:
Instagram: @prettywigstoyou
Facebook: @prettywigstoyou

Heather's next adventure is a subscription box for women and children going through hair loss or cancer treatment. This campaign is being launched on Kickstarter, and people can donate a box to a child or woman with hair loss. A wig will be donated to a child for every 12 boxes sold.

@helperhairbox

Stronger than the Falls

Kim Yoos

When my husband Jim and I were married, we were both young. I was a 22-year-old legal secretary and he was a 24-year-old union floor layer. Our plan was to eventually have a family. After our first year of marriage we threw caution to the wind and decided to let nature take its course. We were excited thinking about the future and making plans. Infertility issues never entered my mind. As time went on and no babies came, I decided to start infertility treatments at age thirty. My life started revolving around blood tests and waiting for results. I felt pretty good when I was actively undergoing treatment, but waiting for results was torture for me and I would basically go on auto pilot. I was worrying my life away and unable to live in the moment. After three miscarriages and countless procedures, we still weren't pregnant. This was an incredibly painful time for me. Jim didn't really get it. He would just try to encourage me that it would happen "when it's supposed to". As much as I wanted to believe that, I was scared I would never have a baby. My anxiety had turned into catastrophic thinking. I finally started seeing a therapist who taught me the tools needed to calm my anxiety. I also reached out to an online support group. It was such a relief to finally be in touch with women who were going through the same things. After several years, we decided to take a break from infertility treatments to explore adoption. I was petrified that we would not be able to adopt. I worried that we would not be approved or we wouldn't be able to afford it. We were at the point in the adoption process where we had to make a considerable down payment. We decided to give IVF one more try. This time, it worked! In June 1999 I was finally pregnant with our daughter Jamie.

The pregnancy was scary for me. I worried that I would miscarry or that something would be wrong with the baby. The triple screen blood test indicated a 1 in 14 chance of Down Syndrome. Considering the circumstances, I felt I needed to know for sure. I had an amnio. The amnio was inconclusive because of blood in the amniotic fluid from a previous bleed I had a few weeks prior. I had a second amnio! Waiting for these results was a nightmare. I took a leave of absence from work. I couldn't think or function. I sat in the living room and watched continuous episodes of 'All in the Family' and just waited for the doctor's call. After waiting for what seemed like forever, we were informed that the baby was a girl and she did not have Down Syndrome. I still remember that phone call. I couldn't speak to the doctor. I was so scared. I made Jim take the call while I hid on the stairs. I literally felt like I was going to collapse when he gave me the news. I was so relieved and happy.

On the morning of March 1, 2000, I sat up in bed and my water broke. After enduring 18 hours of labor the doctor said the baby was in "arrested descent" (meaning she wasn't going anywhere) and I needed a caesarean section. There were lots of emergency c–sections that night so I kept getting pushed to the back of the line since she was not in distress. However, I was in distress...emotional distress! I was super uncomfortable, bed-ridden and highly anxious. After everything we had gone through to get here, I just needed this baby to be born. Finally, they took me in for the c-section and on March 2, 2000 our dreams became a reality. My prayers were answered and at the age of 34 I gave birth to a beautiful baby girl. Three days later we all went home and lived happily ever after... until November 2003.

In 2002 Jim started feeling 'off'. He started having dizzy spells, headaches and bumping into things. I was absolutely terrified and started searching the internet for a diagnosis. Yup, I went straight to Dr. Google. I was convinced he had either a brain tumor, Parkinson's or MS. His doctor sent him for a brain MRI. Thankfully, it came back normal. I was relieved. With this good news we started to think about trying for another child so that Jamie could have a sibling. I really didn't want her to be an only child like I was. To our surprise, I ended up getting pregnant naturally. I was shocked. Because of my previous issues, this was considered a high-risk pregnancy. Everything was progressing normally until I started spotting and then bleeding. I miscarried at 13 weeks. My body failed me once more and I was afraid that if I was ever lucky enough to get pregnant again, I would miscarry. Jim was still having issues. He started seeing all kinds of specialists to get answers. Everything was coming back normal. One doctor suggested that he was simply stressed. Jim was a union floor layer. He loved his job, but it was stressful and he worked a lot. Maybe it was stress. We desperately wanted to believe it was nothing serious. In November 2003, we went ahead with our final IVF and got lucky. I was pregnant again.

In a continuous effort to find out what was going on with Jim, he went to see a neurologist. They sent him for another MRI and requested the original films from the first MRI. The new MRI showed a brain tumor in his cerebellum. The initial "normal" MRI showed the tumor in every single shot. The initial MRI was read wrong (or not read at all). The tumor had been there growing all along. Jim was misdiagnosed! I distinctly remember the day I got the news. Jim was on night work so I took the call. The doctor said he received a copy of the MRI results and Jim had a brain tumor that was "highly concerning". He also stated we needed to see a surgeon immediately. This was ridiculous! We had been told all along that everything was normal! His brain was fine! I was in shock. I had book club that night and I didn't want to go. My girlfriend convinced me to go. I met her in the parking lot of Starbucks and cried in her arms. Pulling myself together, I went into Starbucks and sat through book club. Afterward, I went home and waited up for Jim. I had to tell him that he had a brain tumor all this time and that the initial MRI report was wrong. The following days were spent getting second opinions. The consensus was that the tumor was cancerous. At the next visit with my fertility doctor I had an ultrasound and the doctor told me I was pregnant with twins. I simply said *"I can't be, my husband has brain cancer."* A week later I miscarried.

In January 2004, Jim underwent brain surgery. I sat in the waiting room with Jim's entire family. They were incredibly supportive and with us every step. The operation lasted eight hours. The surgeon informed me that he was able to remove the entire tumor. The next month consisted of trips to the hospital to sit with Jim and advocate for his care. His oldest brother would pick me up around 6:30 every morning and we would go spend the day with Jim. He really couldn't be left alone. He was a fall risk and kept trying to get out of bed. Jim was left with many deficits: severe balance issues, right-sided weakness, speech and short-term memory issues. Jim had to retire from the job he loved. Biopsy results confirmed that the tumor was a rare cancer called Adult

Medulloblastoma. The next few years were filled with doctor visits, chemo, radiation treatments and therapy sessions. Everything had changed. We tried hard to give Jamie a normal life. Family and friends were our backbone and were actively involved in Jim's care. My parents and my aunt were constantly present in our everyday lives. Jamie and I spent a lot of time with playgroup friends; some of whom have become lifelong friends. I once again reached out to online support groups and found one specifically for Adult Medulloblastoma. Connecting to patients and caregivers going through exactly what we were...was lifesaving. I met one online friend in person whose husband had the same cancer. It was so wonderful to meet someone who understood what I was going through as a wife and mother. I knew that I needed to take care of Jim and navigate his situation. However, I still needed to continue to live a happy life, to dream, plan and make memories. Today Jim is doing well. He uses a wheelchair for his balance issues. He has worked hard with physical and occupational therapists. He continues his own exercise program. He is very independent in our own home. We were tremendously fortunate, with the help of Jim's brother, we were able to do a remodel on our home and make it accessible. Jim spends his time exercising, enjoying the gardens and our pool in the summer.

In 2016, I started feeling like something wasn't right. I started getting odd rashes. Then swelling in my ankles and feet. Early summer, my face swelled up and my entire body itched. I went to a local rheumatologist and then a dermatologist who took skin biopsies that indicated possible Lupus. I was put on medication. I also started seeing a naturopathic doctor who did bloodwork, put me on supplements and changed my diet. Nothing was helping. By August, I could no longer work. I was extremely sensitive to fluorescent lights and the sun. I was horribly nauseous, itchy and spent weeks in bed. In December 2016, I started seeing my current doctor at Penn in Philadelphia. He changed up my medication and in April of 2017 I started feeling a little better. I went back to work. Soon, I started having a lot of pain in my joints and I began losing an unhealthy amount of weight. My wrists hurt so badly and my fingers started to curl under. Eventually I couldn't type and I was becoming very weak. I had to stop working again. I was completely terrified that I had some terminal disease. My anxiety was sky high. My family was really concerned, but nobody understood what I was going through, what was happening to me or why the doctors couldn't help. By August 2017, I was extremely underweight. At an appointment with my rheumatologist, he reviewed my blood work and suspected that I didn't have Lupus. Instead, a rare autoimmune disease called Dermatomyositis. Basically, my body was attacking all of my muscles. The only way to definitively diagnose the disease was to have a muscle biopsy. It confirmed the diagnosis. The treatment was high dose IV steroids. I spent nine days in the hospital.

I went home on oral steroids and immunosuppressants. I was under 100 lbs. I couldn't do anything. I was so weak. Physical and occupational therapists came a few times a week. Most days I was so ill I could barely function. It was a struggle to get a meal on the table.

Jamie was headed quickly into adulthood. I felt like I was being robbed of the last few months of motherhood. I agonized over this. I was supposed to be college hunting and filling out college applications. Taking her out to practice driving. Enjoying the events of her last year in high school. Instead, I could barely walk. The muscles in my body were gone. I had no energy. Close friends took her to visit The College of New Jersey. She loved it and eventually committed to it. I had to miss it. Jamie had to take on lots of responsibility. Being an only child, I admit, I spoiled her. She stepped up to the plate and did what was needed. It was a rough time for her watching me waste away, thinking she had one parent in a wheelchair and to now see what was happening to her mom. It was at this time she found a therapist to help her deal with everything.

I just kept getting worse. I was having a hard time swallowing. I was severely weak. I was losing my voice and my speech was affected. I couldn't lift my arms above my head or lift my head off a pillow. My legs felt like they weren't even connected to my body. I looked like a skeleton. I started having trouble breathing. I woke up on October 1, 2017 and knew I needed to get to the hospital. I was admitted with acute respiratory failure and severe malnutrition. I started IVIG infusion. A peg tube was inserted into my stomach and I was hooked up to a feeding pump four times a day. I spent 14 days in the hospital. I was a complete mess. I was out of my head most of the time because of the steroids. I couldn't feed myself. I couldn't get in and out of the bed. My sister-in-law and aunt would come every day to sit with me. Reassuring me that I would be ok. A close friend would check on me. I was afraid to be alone. I couldn't do anything for myself. I was released to a rehab facility where I spent another two weeks. When I was discharged to go home, I felt worse than when I had gone in. At home, I had a nurse and aide twice a week. Occupational and physical therapists came three times a week. I couldn't dress myself, cook, clean or bathe. I was basically helpless. Jim was actually dressing me. Jamie was showering me, doing the food shopping and handling some of the household responsibilities. Neighbors, friends and family took over. My aunt put her own life on hold to care for me and my family. She would come over every night after work, cook dinner for us and do whatever needed to be done. My mom would come over at lunch time. One friend performed Reiki on me throughout my entire illness. Another friend came to cut our hair. Another angel brought me new clothes because mine were too big. Others would come to clean the house or bring meals. I slowly started to put on weight and my muscles started to come back. My peg tube was finally removed in January 2018. Things slowly started to get better.

I have been officially diagnosed with Dermatomyositis, Systemic Scleroderma and Raynaud's Syndrome. I am still on immunosuppressants and receive an infusion every six weeks. I have problems with my hands, wrists, arms and shoulders. My days of being a legal secretary are over. However, I cheer myself on with every new accomplishment! I can now dress myself, drive, get in and out of my car, sing, wash my hair and eat real food! I have once again found an online support group that in the beginning I was afraid to join. I was fearful of what I was going to see. What I see, are warriors! People dealing with pain and suffering. People still finding a way to go on and love their families! I have taken my health into my own hands and actively reduced my stress level. Stress can and does increase my symptoms. Nobody can control that, but me. I am spending my time learning how to meditate (it works wonders). Accessible yoga feels so good and is beneficial for my conditions. My diet is gluten free and low sugar which helps reduce inflammation.

I have met so many wonderful people along this journey. My Rheumatologist and his team at Penn are excellent. The therapists, nurses and aides that helped me along the way are the most caring people; a few have become my personal friends. It is amazing how much good can come into your life from something so devastating. I am grateful. I'm not sure what is ahead in these uncertain times, but I am happy with how far I have come. I recently started my own online support group called *Living Well with Dermatomyositis, Polymyositis, etc.* on Facebook. I encourage anyone going through illness or hard times to search out these online support groups. They have helped me immensely along my journey. I also recently received my Reiki II Certification. I perform Reiki on myself daily and hope to someday share this energy healing with others.

ABOUT KIM YOOS

Kim was raised in Cherry Hill, New Jersey. After graduating high school in 1983; she attended one year of business school and headed straight into the workforce as a legal assistant in a private law firm. She worked in the legal field for 15 years until the birth of her daughter. At that time Kim made the decision to take a step back from work and become a stay-at-home mom. After ten years, Kim returned to the workforce part time at a small law firm where she enjoyed working for the next 8 years until her illness in 2017.

Kim lives in Marlton, New Jersey and enjoys spending time with her family and pets. Currently Kim is working hard at healing her body, mind and spirit through stress reduction, healthy eating, accessible yoga and Reiki. Kim is a Certified Reiki II practitioner.

To connect with Kim through Facebook:

Support group – Living Well with Dermatomyositis, Polymyositis, etc.

Personal page – Kim O'Donnell Yoos

Instagram: kjyoos

Carry my Books and Walk Along Beside Me, Please

Linda O. Carducci

Dear Friend,

On June 20, 2017, my husband of almost 45 years, died peacefully in his bed at our home. Dominick was diagnosed with Lou Gehrig's Disease, also known as ALS (Amyotrophic Lateral Sclerosis) on December 28, 2015. ALS is a neuromuscular disease that affects roughly 30,000 men and women. You can look it up and find that it is a guaranteed heartbreaker of a disease. When the doctor says *"All indications are that you have Amyotrophic Lateral Sclerosis, otherwise known as Lou Gehrig's Disease"*, it is shockingly paralyzing. Time stops. Disbelief takes over. Bargaining begins. Odds are you have never known someone actually delivered of such a diagnosis. Odds are you have been chasing a diagnosis for about a year and you were prepared for a nasty disease with a difficult passage to a cure. In our case, Dominick had endured a dozen years of dealing with bladder cancer, larynx cancer, twenty-five bouts of sepsis, kidney issues and serious DVTs. We knew how to fight. He knew how to fight. It doesn't take long for the reality of the diagnosis to hit. No cure. No remission. No relief from the relentless deterioration of muscles in the legs, the arms, the mouth, the throat, the lungs, excessive saliva production, swallowing challenges and feeding tubes. No reprieve. In many cases, there is no lingering in this life. So, in the midst of the tests, machines for breathing issues, machines to clear saliva, machines to shake phlegm from the throat, appointments, hospital beds, wheel chairs, Hoyer lifts, speech machines, drinking and eating issues...there is the pervasive knowing this was the war that couldn't be won. The only battles to be fought were for safety and comfort. These were battles of significance.

We trudged through the myriad of tests, doctors, physical therapy, changing medications, struggle to get a diagnosis and referral to the ALS Clinic. Struggling with foot lifts, wheel chairs, walkers, uncertainty and frustration; we relied on friends and family for comfort combined with concern. Everyone said to let them know if we needed anything. Really? Would the well-meaning offers give us the impossible? We began the journey of learning what it means to endure. We thought we knew and understood what it meant to endure; but quickly discerned the difference between enduring treatments to a recovery and the consequences of an incurable disease with no hope of recovery.

Church was hard. Dominick reestablished his relationship with the Catholic Church and, for as long as he could manage it, rolled into the specially equipped van graciously provided by a family member to attend Mass on Sundays. When possible, one of his daughters joined him. On Sundays, when he had company, I went to my church until I couldn't bear the emotional tug that turned to tears and the questions that had no good answers. Marie, a fellow Nurture Guide, gently said *"Oh, you have started the grieving process."* I hadn't thought of it in quite that way, but it was true. The grieving started long before the death.

I read everything, devouring information about ALS, about complications, accommodations, caregiving, options and about the grief that accompanies the entire process. I joined online groups and created online friendships with others who were also diagnosed with and battling ALS. I joined online groups for caregivers and web-based support groups. Later, I joined groups of other widows and widowers who shared experiences and feelings. Some were helpful; others not so much. Over time, I discontinued those that didn't benefit me; but I tried everything I found.

How do you get through? How can others help? You can walk along beside and carry my books. What does that mean? Obviously, not a literal request, because no one can walk the path for you. However, they can walk beside you. They can't carry the burden of the caregiving or the grief, but they can help ease the weight of the *"books"*. Every bit of advice for getting through includes being able to draw on community. What is community? It is your family members, your neighbors, your church or spiritual family, your work community, along with the medical community and others who work within the associations or governmental agencies of aging and disabilities. It is the receptionist at the doctor's office, the pharmacist, the clerk at the grocery store, your housekeeper, gardener and mail person. It is the friend who sends you a comical instant message daily for a year to give you a reason to smile. It is others who are also on the journey. You need each of them as you stumble down the path of pain. Unfortunately, for many of the community, grief and death isn't part of their vocabulary. They don't mean to be unkind or uncaring…they just don't have the words. They will ask how you feel, what they can do, how they can help…all while rushing out the door and hoping you won't really answer the questions. They won't bring up your lost loved one's name and either go silent or chatter to hide their discomfort.

Then, there are those who will walk beside you. They show up. They bring you coffee, meals, cards and flowers. Sometimes they bring you communion and prayers of comfort. They answer a text immediately and listen as you talk about the past, share your stories and validate your love. They come to plant the flowers you bought and couldn't bring yourself to plant. They come and weed the garden, take out the trash, dust and run a vacuum. They are there, walking beside you and carrying what part of the burden they can. They laugh and cry with you or sit in silence as you rock yourself into calm. They run interference with others who sincerely want to 'help', but don't know how. They pass along information so you don't have to repeat yourself or stop what you are doing to answer the same question a gazillion times. They help you tell your story.

After the death, the wake, funeral and cemetery...they give you room, but never close the door. Here are some of the things I came to understand; at the heart and soul level.

When someone asks how you are feeling, they can't really understand. Unless they have suffered through a traumatic loss themselves, they don't have the framework to understand how you might be feeling. *Might* is the operative word. We each push through life and its challenges in our own unique way. We don't love or grieve in the same way as any other person. Grief counselors notwithstanding, not everyone goes through the recognized five stages of grief. These are usually presented as:

- Stage 1: Shock and denial
- Stage 2: Anger
- Stage 3: Bargaining
- Stage 4: Depression and detachment
- Stage 5: Acceptance

This staging is misleading and only barely helpful when you are struggling with brain fog and confusion. You don't wake up and say *"OK, done with shock and denial, now onto 'anger'."* What if you are never angry? Does that mean you are stuck and will never move past shock and denial? I always thought the stages of grief would be more accurately visualized as a spinning wheel that includes each of the emotional states. From moment to moment, hour to hour, and day to day...we experience these emotional states. Maybe we experience them for the rest of our lives. The wheel is always turning. Why do we even need to name these stages? Frankly, it helps us and others keep our sanity during insane, or otherwise impossible times. Helping us to recognize the color and nature of the collection of feelings and resulting behaviors we will endure as we live our loss.

Another thing I've come to understand, is that even those who rally round during the caregiving and funeral times may move away. They resume their lives, perhaps changed a bit; but essentially the same as before your trauma. You resume living as well, but it isn't the life you had, or dreamed of or planned to have. Nothing is recognizable. You are told you will *'get over it'* and *'move on'*. There might be mention of your lost love being in *'a better place'*, or *'there is a reason'* and even an *'I know how you feel.'* After some time, people might even be unaware enough to ask you how long you're going to continue with this grieving and *'hasn't it been long enough?'* They might act as if you are wallowing in self-pity, proceeding to tell you a story about how they overcame a similar loss and moved on. Wow! I believe strongly in authenticity and I know the power of telling your story out loud; but your story, your reaction, your response and your grief path is yours alone. Heaven knows it isn't mine.

If there is ever a time when you need to protect your heart; this is it. Surround yourself with people who love you. You need a place for soft landings. That might be your church, synagogue or temple. It might be the gym, or a beautiful garden, a hiking path or the swing set in the backyard. Sit in a favorite chair, smell his aftershave (I squirted Dominick's favorite 'Joop' on our pillows after his scent was gone), cover yourself in the prayer shawl that he found comforting, wear his robe or shirts. Do what will bring you comfort and try not to be overcome with hurt when the very people who should be comforting you don't come around, don't call, don't return calls and just move on. Their neglect isn't on you; it's on them. Acknowledge the hurt as real and let them take responsibility for it.

Your primary responsibility is to yourself. It might seem selfish, but so be it. It's about priority management. We can't really manage time. We may not have much control over external events, but we can be deliberate and conscientious about our intentions. Do what you need to do to work through the pain while dealing with the life stuff of taking care of kids, a house, the laundry, dusting, vacuuming, grocery shopping, meals, a car, a job, the estate and finances. Try not to allow anyone else to tell you what you 'need to do', especially if it doesn't resonate with you. If you don't already know how to say 'thank you for your concern and advice' without committing to anything, practice now. If you question advice, pause. Give yourself time to push through your foggy thinking and the inevitable indecision to an answer you can own.

The brain fog will lift. When? When you are ready and not one minute longer. When will you be sure your decisions are sound? When you are sure and not one minute sooner. While you wade through the muck; try to remember to get rest, eat balanced meals, bathe, get out of your jammies and do 'normal' things. There is comfort in ritual. Allow yourself to cry. Never apologize for your tears and try not to 'stuff' them. Stuffing emotions is one pathway to PTSD (post-traumatic stress disorder).

As part of making yourself a priority, try not to neglect your health. Sudden and unexpected loss can affect us as much as prolonged caregiving or a lingering death. You can expect physical responses to the mental and emotional stresses of grief. Conditions you might have been monitoring can be exacerbated by the excess of cortisol. The list of symptoms is long and some can easily be overlooked as a 'normal' reaction to grief. Unfortunately, prolonged stress can lead to cardiovascular, neurological and auto-immune distress. Just as an example, my BP elevated, my HR slowed, my rhythms became erratic, I fell multiple times (no focus) resulting in a stenosis and requiring PT, I was diagnosed with poly-neuropathy, had a heart stent placement and am facing a renal artery stinting. I have experienced numerous skin reactions and rashes. All were unexpected consequences of too much stress and too much pain.

There are hundreds of books, websites and groups about grief, loss, caregiving and surviving loss. The author whose work resonated most clearly with me is Gary Roe. Gary isn't a medical doctor or a psychiatrist. He works in Hospice and tells his story of multiple losses while sharing experiences encountered during the course of his work. His books are short (a real blessing when you have limited focus), poignant and sincere. I have read and listened to many books over the past years, but Gary's books have been my favorites.

If you have suffered a loss that shakes your life…my heart hurts for you. I can't say I understand your pain, but I am here for you. As best I can, *I will walk beside you and carry your books.*

Much love,
Linda

Illustrations by Monica Roa Szwarcberg © 123RF.com

ABOUT LINDA O. CARDUCCI

Linda lives in Northern Virginia with her nephew and senior puppy, Lucky. She has a passion for service, for travel (especially to Italy!), singing, painting, sewing, reading, writing and learning.

After many years in various professions, including banking, construction, real estate brokerage and residential property management; she now offers coaching and mentoring to individuals and small companies when not volunteering.

She is working on an exciting memoir of her late husband and looks forward to sharing his fantastic story with the world. Linda is honored to share her story of living with and through the grief of losing her husband to ALS in 2017.

Out of the Darkness

Amanda Kijek

When I was a little girl, I never really dreamed of playing with dolls or the newest, trendiest, must have toys. All I thought about was having my sister close. Making sure she felt safe and happy. Don't get me wrong, I had toys and probably favorites, but nothing that stood out in my mind. Nothing that acted as a security blanket of sorts. To me, security came in the form of my little sister's smile and closeness.

For me, life started out like I would imagine is familiar to most. A mom and dad. Grandparents to visit on the weekends. My parents had my sister and myself less than a year apart and then they divorced. That part wasn't so bad, because I really grew up not knowing any different. My sister and I lived with mom. My dad's job required that he worked far away and that pattern continued my entire childhood. So, it was just the three of us (mom, my sister and me) and I was a happy little girl, content with it that way.

I remember the day it all changed. I would have been only about five or six years old at the time. It seemed like out of nowhere my mom started packing boxes and clothes. Although she might have mentioned we were moving to a new city, it never became clear until my favorite bike with the multi colored tassels that floated in the breeze as I rode in front of our duplex, was sold for extra money towards the move. Thinking back, I can understand the pressure my mom must have been under to support my sister and I on her single income, the uncertainty of a move to a new city, a new apartment and new job. She was an independent woman. As an adult now, I can understand why her usual chill demeanor seemed forced and she carried an extra burden on her. I would miss my bike, but I trusted her when she said we would get another. The new duplex was similar to the one we had left. Bedrooms upstairs with the living room and kitchen on the main floor. I remember my strawberry shortcake curtains and bedding. I remember feeling pretty excited about the huge park and nearby school that were both in walking distance. It checked all the boxes on my list and I was happy. Until, the man moved in.

I recognized him as someone I had seen my mom with at work before. He was big and looked happy all the time. He would play little card games with me and my sister. He would let us win a dollar from him and I didn't mind him around at first. It wasn't long after we had moved that I started the first grade. I would come home to his friends drinking and loud music playing. They would seem happy to see my sister and I. They would always let us play card games and let us win of course. We would make as much as we could in the dollar wins so that we could run to the nearby store and buy candy. We had a pretty good system, I thought. One day, after school, it seemed louder and everyone seemed to be extra. Extra yelling. Extra singing. Extra dancing. EXTRA everything. My mom was home from work already and was quick to greet us. She immediately sent us upstairs to play. The night seemed to go on forever. I remember my sister and I being scared to even come out of our room to go to the bathroom to pee. The energy was so dark and heavy. Even through the loudly blared music, the shouting and crashes of furniture with broken glass seemed to somehow still rise above. Once we finally gathered the courage to dart to the bathroom, that was directly at the top of the staircase, it seemed like everything went instantly quiet and time slowed down. It was like that crazy tunnel vortex when you see everything happening right before your eyes, but can't do anything about it. Both my mom and the man were somehow right there on the stairs. Here we were, stranded between the bathroom and our room. With the time warp tunnel of how to get back to our room before getting in trouble. However, we weren't in trouble, my mom was. The man was pushing and grabbing at her. She was trying to get away and get upstairs. I could see she was scared. When she saw us, she yelled for us to run to our room and lock the door. I'll never forget the sound of his fists connecting and her crying as she pleaded for him to stop. That was the first time I witnessed a man hitting a woman. Someone who was laughing and having fun only hours before. I didn't understand what my mom did to provoke it. What I did understand was that I could never trust the man again and I would try my hardest to never let my mom be hurt by him again. Things quieted down, almost instantly, after my mom made it upstairs and into her room. He seemed to give up. My sister and I listened for a while on the other side of our bedroom door until we thought we could make the exit safely to get to our mom's room. Once inside, we quietly closed the door and crawled into bed next to her. She stunk with the same sour like smells we recognized from the man's friends who partied here all the time, but I didn't care...I snuggled in close.

The fights seemed to become more and more frequent. My mom had taught me how to dial a special number that sent a cab and it would take us to a safe place where we could stay. There were lots of other women who looked bruised, beaten and defeated; just like my mom. We would always stay a few days and then she would always go back to him. Sometimes, when we didn't call the cab, the neighbors must have heard the noise and called the police. They would show up at our door, but my mom would always say everything was ok. She looked so frightened. I don't know why they believed her.

I wanted to yell out what the man was doing to her, but I was scared what would happen to my mom if I told. One morning, I went downstairs after another crazy night and I remember seeing him lying on the couch. There were cuts all over his arms and blood everywhere. I wished and wished he was dead, but he wasn't. I never gave up hoping.

My sister and I would walk to school. It would seem so nice to walk amongst the other kids, playing and talking. It was as if we were in another life. Like the bloody mess of a living room wasn't even there. We would talk about grandma and grandpa's farm. About playing in the garden and making each other laugh. It was my favorite time with her. I couldn't wait for school to be over to talk and play with her again. One day, as if our dreams were being answered, my grandparents showed up at our school. I hadn't felt that happy in a long time. My grandma said she didn't know where we were and she was so worried about us. She had managed to track us down by calling the schools in the area of the city she thought we were in. Thankfully she got in touch with someone who told her we were there and safe.

The next thing I remember, my mom sent us to be with grandma and grandpa. She said she couldn't come because of her job and our house. I worried about her everyday…staying where the man was. No one could ever understand what she was going through the way my sister and I did. There was no way I could make anyone understand the way they needed to, after all, I was only a child. The next few years were a custody battle between my dad, who was remarried, and my grandparents. There were lawyers and psychiatrists. It seemed like these people who were supposed to be so smart...just wouldn't listen to anything I told them. My sister and I wanted to live with our grandparents. They were always around and we had friends our age in a school nearby. We loved our dad and understood he wanted to be part of our lives, but we had never lived with him before. My stepmom was very unfair, always taking sides with her kids over us and she was physically mean to my sister. I hated her so much and she knew it. She would slap my sister or knock frying pans into her face as she was drying them for her chores. Once she even sat on my sister's little body, pinning her down to burn her hand with a lighter, as a way of teaching her a lesson for playing with matches. She never did any of this when my dad was around, but then again, he was always away working...so he never knew. I got tired of trying to tell people what I wanted. I hated seeing my sister miss our mom and be bullied by one that she only wanted affection from. I felt like my main priority was my sister, her safety and her happiness. It was nice to see her make friends so easily over the years. She easily could have become closed off, like I was beginning to do. I felt angry all the time and became so tough. More like a little boy than a girl. I was strong, athletic and didn't have more than one friend at a time. I talked back and hit back if my stepmom did anything to my sister or myself. It was hard for me to trust anyone or make friends. When I did, it was always in my mind, I didn't want to get too close. I wasn't planning on being around there too much longer. I am still grateful to this day, for the one friend I made that kept me grounded and sympathized with me (as much as she could for kids our age). She and her family were my hard line to what normal kids' lives should be like. Without that, my stubbornness to do things on my own and not trust anyone but my sister or grandparents, would have broken my spirit and pulled me into the darkness.

After a few years of ongoing court battles and the passing of my grandpa; my grandma got custody of us. She was so strong to lose her husband, bring in two pre-teens and raise us. The entire time she still worked at getting my mom closer and straightened out. Eventually building her a home only a couple miles down the road from us. Everything was falling into place and life had never been better. I graduated and moved to the nearest city to attend college. I became a young working adult with all the responsibilities and making my own life choices on my own terms. I found myself doing things I enjoyed; like joining volleyball teams and going to the gym. I even opened up and made some great friendships. I found myself falling in love.

I had been through enough over the years to know the importance of a healthy mind and a strong support system. Watching and learning from my grandma as she leaned on the community. Watching as she continually grew emotionally, mentally, spiritually and physically to be the best version of herself. My experiences helped cultivate a deep understanding of integrity and moral importance. Even though I had this understanding within myself; I would find myself replaying situations similar to my mom's relationships in my own love life. I married young, was cheated on repeatedly and tried to fix it. Once I checked in with myself and I recognized the triggers; I walked out. It was the hardest thing I had to do as an adult. It meant leaving a mortgage and the things I worked hard for. I even had to leave the recently renovated salon and spa I was working hard designing with my business partner. The hardest part for me was asking for help from my friends and my family. Knowing that I would now need to rely on others. Knowing that I would have to own up to this failure as a wife and a business owner. It's something I knew from my life experiences to search out help; to strengthen through trainings and mindset work.

No woman should settle for less than her dreams. Thanks to my grandmother's example, my family and friends support, and the time I invested into mentors and training...I realized that no one can ever take anything from you; unless you let them. Today, I have a healthy relationship with my mom. She is remarried to a wonderful man that treats her how a woman should be treated. I am happily married to my best friend and biggest supporter. I am a mom of two toddlers, whom I get to spend my days with, because I can work from home and on a schedule I control. I have created courses and programs to help busy moms create an income from home so that they can live life on their own terms as well. I have a growing Facebook community; specifically created for accountability, support and guidance for determined women in network marketing through simplified business building strategies and the strong foundation they need to sustain success.

ABOUT AMANDA KIJEK

Amanda Kijek resides in Alberta Canada; where she is a fulfilled mom of two and happily married to her best friend.

She has been a small business owner, helping women see themselves as the goddesses they are, for over 15 years. More recently, in the past 4.5 years, she has taken her work online. This allows her to control her schedule and be a full-time parent, which is what is most important to her. She works alongside online marketers who want to see their businesses surge and provides them coaching or consulting services. Her 15 years' experience in the home business industry has given her a broad base from which to approach many scenarios. She especially enjoys working with network marketing professionals who want to add coaching to their own repertoire.

Amanda contributes content regularly to https://www.facebook.com/AmandaKijek

Her content focuses on the most up-to-date business building information. Utilizing organic Facebook strategies and attraction marketing methods, but never at the expense of providing a clear and simplified approach busy women can apply with ease.

Learn more how Amanda's coaching and how it could grow your business by booking your free breakthrough session at https://amandakijek.com/schedule/

Just A Girl Who Decided to Go for It

Gretel Leach

I was born in 1986. I grew up with my parents and my younger brother in a small town called Burntwood; located in Staffordshire United Kingdom. I had a very normal upbringing; my parents were great role models to my brother and me. The family home was always full of warmth, laughter and love. I have some very fond memories of my childhood and growing up.

My mom always made sure that we had a proper dinner on the table each night, that we had clean clothes to wear, and that the house was clean and tidy; she did everything she could as a mother to provide us with a happy and healthy life. My dad was like a warm blanket who I would go to for advice and support. He would always have his ear ready to listen and knew exactly what to say to make things better. Both of my parents worked very hard to provide for the family financially. I always had love, stability and support.

My brother was a quiet lad and would usually keep to himself while playing on his computer. I preferred it that way, so I knew he wasn't out on the streets and up to no good.

Throughout my upbringing, I was conditioned to always do the *right* things; get a career so I was self-sufficient. Most importantly, I was conditioned to always think about what other people would think of me if I did the *wrong* things. The conditioning came from a place of love, but it led me to completely cover up who I truly was in efforts to please others. I was constantly worrying what other people were thinking of the way I spoke, the way I looked and the way I lived my life. This accumulated over time and by the time I reached age 15; I felt something starting to bubble away, like this feeling of wanting to do the opposite of what I was supposed to do.

I started going out after school drinking and getting up to no good. It was exciting and the opposite of what I was "supposed" to be doing. I enjoyed it because I felt free from what was normal and acceptable. It allowed that rebel in me to come out. So, I spent the next few years doing exactly what I thought I should *not* be doing, but having a whale of a time whilst doing it. There was alcohol, all night spent at clubs I wasn't old enough to get in and you can imagine the rest! However, at the time, I had this constant battle in my head saying: *"you should not be doing this; what are other people going to say when they find out."* I covered up my regret, shame and guilt by doing the same things repeatedly; because it was my only escape from the reality that I faced. I felt that I had to be perfect in order to be accepted. This caused me to suffer severe social anxiety; because in my head, I was living a double life.

At the age of 23, I met my ex-partner who I remained with for six years. Within the first 12 months of being together we were already having arguments and it became clear very quickly that we triggered each other, but I wanted the relationship to work. We spent our weekends drinking and doing what we could to numb ourselves. We didn't do the normal things that couples do like going out for meals or to the movie cinema. After a few years of being together; we decided to move in together. It didn't quite work out how I had imagined. I found myself with no money most of the time and dreading the weekends because I often ended up on my own. That's when the arguments became really bad. The relationship felt mentally and emotionally controlling. It was the darkest time of my life because I felt trapped. My mind and body were screaming at me to get out, but something kept me there. I often sat on the sofa at home crying because I was so unhappy.

Looking back, there was no Gretel in that chapter of my life. It was all about my partner and how I could support him. I had completely neglected the most important person, me. I continued covering up my unhappiness and insecurities. He did the same. This just created a very volatile relationship. After about 18 months, I plucked up the courage to leave and go back to my mom. It felt so good to be home and like a weight had been lifted off my shoulders. You would have thought I would have known the relationship wasn't right by then, however, I stayed with him for another three years after that. We both continued to self-sabotage and it was around the last few years of the relationship that I really started to feel depressed about my whole life. I constantly felt this heavy knot in my stomach; full of guilt and shame about who I had become. I had lost all respect and love for myself a long time ago. I wanted out of this lifestyle so badly, but trying to break free from all that I had known for a big chunk of my life was not easy. We spilt up a few times after that, but always got back together. In August 2016, we split up for the last time and I eventually found the courage to say goodbye to the relationship. In saying goodbye, I also said goodbye to the lifestyle that was making me so miserable.

I don't blame him for anything. I take full responsibility for my life at that time. I had my shit to deal with and he had his. I know now that he came into my life for a reason and I don't regret a single day of the relationship. We had some good times, but the bad times outweighed the good. That's okay though, as it was always meant to be that way. I learned how I want to be as a person and the kind of partner I want to be with. Those lessons were invaluable. Making the decision to take back my own life was hard, but nothing could have prepared me for what was to come.

Once I had stopped using my lifestyle to escape from my own fears and insecurities; it opened me up for the world to see. My anxiety was the worst it had ever been and I struggled on a daily basis with debilitating physical symptoms such as a racing heart, tremors, sweating, dizziness and blushing. I had a total lack of confidence in myself and extremely low self-esteem. The mental battle between this perfect girl I thought I should be and the reality of the life I had lived for so long, haunted me every day.

First thing I started doing was journaling about my thoughts and feelings. I also began reading books on social anxiety. I started dipping my toes into the spiritual side of things and realized soon afterwards that I was an empath. It was as if a lightbulb went off for me. It all made complete sense as to why I had always felt so different towards other people. Why I always wanted to help people. Why I was a massive people pleaser at the expense of my own needs. It explained a lot about why I put up with so much in my previous relationship. I had no boundaries and I said yes to everybody for fear of being judged or worse yet, not accepted.

Six months after leaving my previous relationship, I met my current partner. That is when all of my fears and insecurities were illuminated for me to see. At first, I even struggled to have a meal with him. I could not bear the eye contact and in my head, I felt as though I was being constantly judged. There were a couple of occasions where I just felt completely unworthy of his time, energy and any social things we did together. I turned to alcohol as my comfort blanket. Every time I had a conversation with him over the telephone, I feared I might say something silly and be laughed at or judged. This was a daily battle for me. I finally decided to speak to the doctors and they put me forward for Cognitive Behavioral Therapy. It helped a bit and for a limited time, but it still did not change my energy and mindset around how I looked at myself. The shame, guilt, regret, unworthiness and fear were all still there.

In 2017, the daily battle of trying to be strong took its toll on me and I had a breakdown. I remember that day so clearly. I felt this sudden panic come over me like I could not go on without some sort of relief from the suffering I endured on a daily basis. I sobbed to my partner on the phone who's only words of comfort were: "I would never normally tell somebody to consider medication, but I really feel this is the only option for you right now." That was my lowest point.

Along with the anxiety...I felt depressed as well. I was put on an anti-anxiety medication and began seeing a counsellor. The medication was an absolute lifesaver and I could not have carried on without it at the time. However, I didn't want to stay on the medication. I knew it was not getting me to the root of my problems. Instead, it was only covering them up. So along with the help of my counselling sessions, after about six months, I gradually weened myself off them. The deep feeling of dread and fear came back. I continued with the self-help journaling, meditating, yoga, reading books and then the universe started putting spiritual teachers into my path. That's when my coach came along.

I had never even heard of a "coach" before, but when I spoke to her something far beyond my logical mind became the driving force in what would be the most life changing decision I would ever make. That driving force was my soul and it was urging me to make this decision. To make a commitment to myself. Apart from my ego screaming at me, I grabbed the bull by its horns and said yes! It was a four-month program, but I ended up working with my coach for 10 months altogether. It dramatically changed my life. I completely reprogrammed my mindset from a place of regret, shame and guilt to a place of gratitude and love for every single person or experience that had come into my life. I shifted my energy around my self-confidence and self-esteem. I gradually started to blossom into the person that I had forgotten even existed.

I can't explain the feeling you get when you start to heal yourself; letting go of suppressed emotions and fears. It is truly liberating and joyful. The program also awakened my spiritual gifts. It opened up the door to my soul's purpose in helping other women, who are like me, to free themselves from limiting beliefs along with fear and to reclaim their power back.

During all this time of grit, determination and transformation my partner was a massive part of my healing journey. He held space for me at my lowest point to try and find myself again. He allowed me to be vulnerable again and supported me when I was feeling scared or alone. He is so special to me and I will always remember how he was there for me in my darkest times. My soulmate, my savior and my world. I love him from a place that is indescribable. It is a feeling that comes when you meet the missing part of your soul and the bond we share is unbreakable.

I am now completely free from the shackles of anxiety and I live a happy life with solid boundaries in place. I am living my truth and I have taken back my power. I am an untethered boss of my life all because I decided to go for it and say yes to me! I have continued to work with other coaches since starting my healing journey and I am becoming a more evolved version of myself every single day. I would easily say that my favorite thing in the whole wide world is to be alone, away from the hustle and bustle of life, so I can listen to what my body and soul is trying to tell me. A few years ago, that would have been nearly impossible for me; because being alone reminded me that I was still this girl who had made the wrong choices and done things that I was not proud of. This girl that was not worthy of love, not worthy of a nice home, not worthy of being like everybody else...all because I had chosen to do things that were not accepted by other people. I have now worked through all of the conditioning and the limiting beliefs about who I thought I should be. I feel like I have been set free. Free as the wind. Able to live for me unapologetically and unconditionally. To live for what makes me happy, what makes me tick and what lights me up instead of what makes somebody else happy.

The last 10 years of my life I have studied and trained in law to become a Chartered Legal Executive, a lawyer for anybody who doesn't know what that is. I have worked in property for the last seven years and it may sound fancy to you thinking...I am a lawyer, but honestly it bores the life out of me. It was just another avenue I took in my life because getting a career in law was seen as really respected by others and a good way to earn money. It's the most soul-destroying job there is. You work your arse off for people to turn around and say you are not doing it quick enough. Thankfully, I now know what it is I am here to do. I am so passionate about helping other women to be happy and to live their best life. I am highly grateful for my career, for many reasons, I just know that it isn't for me.

This journey is just incredible and I want you to know that it is available to everybody; but it starts with you making that decision to invest in yourself and your happiness.

You come first and then everything else will follow.

ABOUT GRETEL LEACH

Gretel Leach was born and raised in Staffordshire United Kingdom. At the age of 22 she started studying law and qualified as a Chartered Legal Executive at the age of 27. She loves hot yoga and trains Brazilian jujitsu with her partner Jon. She is currently residing in Staffordshire United Kingdom with her partner Jon and fur baby Archie. She enjoys spending time with Jon over some nice food and fine wine.

Gretel owns her own business as an Intuitive Anxiety Coach where she helps women to go from a lack of confidence and persistent fear to reclaiming their power and their sparkle back. She is a spiritual leader, an emotional, intuitive and mirroring empath. She is claircognizant and clairsentient. Gretel uses her spiritual gifts to catapult her clients from their deepest darkest fears into their red-hot power! Her specialty is helping other women to completely free themselves from the shackles of anxiety so that they can be happy and live in their truth. She has a passion for energy work and that is what makes her different from any other Anxiety Coach out there! Gretel will always tell you that everything is energy and that is exactly what anxiety is, just energy. She is passionate about helping women that are in the position she was and she has years of experience suffering with severe social anxiety herself; making her able to stand in the shoes off her clients.

To connect with Gretel, please visit
Website: www.you-1st.co.uk

Facebook: Private page – Gretel Leach

Business page –
https://www.facebook.com/YourIntuitiveAnxietyCoach/

Girl, Don't Fall on Your Face

Emily Blake

Blinding beautiful bikinis. Heels tall enough that with just one wrong step, you *could* actually die. Bright iridescent lights that make everything so magical. Tanned strong bodies everywhere I looked. All I could think about was *"what am I doing here?"*. I didn't belong among all these amazing humans, yet I chose this. I chose to compete in a fitness competition called the *Fitness Atlantic*. At first glance, to someone outside of this world, you could think it is just another beauty pageant. Right? Just step-up on-stage half naked and parade around while getting judged on how you look. At least that's what my husband's first reaction was when I told him about my plan: *"You want to do what now?"*. Never in my wildest dreams did I truly understand what it took to get to this moment. The transformation that would occur; the healing of mind, body and spirit. The months of preparation, the hours in the gym, the commitment needed to pull off this crazy dream, the posing practices that never did soften my awkwardness and my goodness the endless amounts of cardio just for a few minutes of showcasing all my hard work to the world. I had such a deep sense of gratitude for everyone there. Each of them needed to be applauded. Not because they were better or more deserving, but because like a phoenix rising from the ashes, each of them should be regarded as uniquely remarkable.

Up on stage, my mind had the craziest of commentaries when it came to seeing myself in the same light as I saw the others. A different story all together. I would hear *"Wow, girl, you are such an inspiration"* or *"You are amazing, you look so good"*. They couldn't be saying that about me? I didn't accept compliments like these very well. I would tell myself that they were just trying to make me feel good. My mind was telling me: if I believe their words, it will make me somehow shallow or arrogant. I have learned, that our mind plays the worst tricks on us. They are lies we tell ourselves to conform to what society, family and friends expect us to believe. That we are not pretty enough to do something like this. That we are not strong enough or courageous enough to achieve the dreams we have envisioned for ourselves. This just isn't the case; I know with every fiber of my being that if I can do it...so can you. My experiences, my struggles and my strengths are up to me to make. As I was up there, fully immersed in this experience, with no way out...my thoughts shifted. *Girl, yes, I can accept that I am inspiring*...it doesn't change how I treat people. It doesn't change who I am or who I want to be. What it does change, is my energy and vibration. What I have accomplished is unapologetically stayed in the pursuit of my dreams and I have proven to others that they can do the same. That revelation alone, would be the catalyst to a wonderful future.

We all have a story to tell, a perspective that might resonate with someone one day and give them hope or light. It's my prayer, that people reading my story, know that no matter the struggles we face...you are not alone and can achieve anything you put your mind to do. Your dream may not be walking across a stage in five-inch heels and equally deathly afraid of falling on your face. However, each and every one of you reading this today, you have a dream.

Now, let me bring you back to about seven years ago, when I was blind. Not literally, but figuratively. When I had what some would say was a "good life". I was with my then husband for 15 years, had two beautiful energetic boys, a stable job at the hospital, good friends and a house that we had just purchased. I was finishing up school to be a massage therapist. Not that bad, right? I had grown up in a strong military family. One that encouraged me to cultivate all areas of my life: creatively, intellectually and socially. So, it is hard looking back to find myself in the position I was in. I had lived overseas in Spain. I had attained my black belt. I had competed in multiple discipline competitions like shooting and archery. I even won the CT state art award. So many things in my life that should have suggested I was capable of being strong and happy. When my eyes couldn't disregard the little things any longer; I started connecting the dots in my day to day life. No longer was I able to go through the motions of the day blindly. For instance, my husband meeting a girl at a bar and using the excuse to me that everyone else from work didn't show up. Really? Or the cold shoulder, when his phone would incessantly keep pinging. Who the heck could you be talking to at this hour? The increased amount of yelling and arguments about nothing truly important. No, it was just in my head. We had been together for far too long for our marriage to be anything other than normal.

I started to analyze everything and just like every woman does…we start to criticize ourselves first. Yeah, maybe I put on too much weight. He must not find me attractive anymore. Ok, more like fifty pounds too much. Maybe we are going through this hard time because I don't shave my legs every day. Maybe it was that I don't talk that much. Honestly, who wants to talk when they are tired? Most men would appreciate a quiet wife. I didn't nag or like yelling. All the words that come from his mouth on a consistent basis about how horrible I was: *"You don't cook," "this house is a mess," "what, are you stupid or something,"* and *"you can't do anything right."* When you hear those things, over and over again, it starts to recondition your brain like you would by reprogramming a computer. I couldn't help, but start to believe them.

I remember the day so clearly, the day my whole world came tumbling down like a stack of playing cards. It was eight o'clock in the morning and I was on my way to take my final practical exam for massage school. I was nervous and excited. I mean I had finally made it to the end of that semester! I even remember thinking to myself *"damn girl...you juggled nightshift, no sleep, family, and school...you are one bad bitch"*. I deserved to feel happy. Then, my phone started ringing. It was from a couple that I had become very close with. The voice on the other end saying *"Emily, I am so sorry, but your husband is definitely cheating on you. I have proof."* How could one phone call change everything? My stomach went into my throat. Everything stood still even while I was driving. I had a million emotions. A guilty sense of relief that my suspicions were finally validated. A sense of betrayal, anger and confusion. I was completely and utterly devastated. How could someone who you vowed to be with, love unconditionally and had always accused me of cheating, do something like that? I was dumbfounded. Then the tears came, oh the tears, it was like an ugly cry. A purge of fifteen years built up that was finally finding its way out. What was happening? I still don't know how I made it to school that day without any accidents occurring. My dear friends consoled me the best they could. My passing grade, which I still suspect was a pity pass, but I took it.

The next few months were a whirlwind and I am still unsure how I managed to stay sane. I had kicked my husband out of the house and changed the locks, which I now know was illegal, oops. I found myself feeling unsafe and protecting my kids became my biggest priority. The hole in the wall from his recent outburst only motivated me more. Divorce was the only course of action in my mind. If my upbringing taught me anything, it was that when you are faced with an impossible decision, you just close your eyes and do exactly what your gut instincts tell you to do. I had made the right choice; granted it was probably the last right choice I would make in a long time. I let our new house, that I worked so hard to get, go into foreclosure with almost everything that we had left in it. I just had to get out of there. It symbolized everything wrong in my life. Now a single mom and facing how I would handle money, childcare and just survival...I had so many questions I needed to find answers for...and find them fast.

I became depressed. Withdrawing from reality. When the kids were away at either their nanas or grandmothers; I found solace in alcohol, cigarettes and sex. I felt very raw, like a gaping wound that couldn't be cauterized. I wanted to feel whole again somehow, some way. Who had I become? How did I turn into this person? I lost friends, people that I cared about and had trusted. Would this darkness ever end? Lonely and abandoned, I just couldn't see the goodness in anything anymore. Suicide, which I had thought of so many times as the easy way out. Now, it had become more of an option. I found myself one night at the emergency room pleading for help. I felt judgement emanating from the medical staff as they looked from the kids to myself. I worked in the medical field for far too long to not pick up on the little nuances. I just couldn't get through this. While sitting there, looking into the eyes of my boys, I knew I couldn't leave them like that. They were my only saving grace. My sweet angels. It upset me to think about them having to be subjected to all this uncertainty and unbalance. I had to change. I had to pull myself together for them. They deserved better and so did I.

After getting some help, I came to the decision that it was time to find myself again. I started using the time I had to further my education and head back to the gym. I made a silent commitment to myself that no one will dictate my life any longer. I will no longer allow peoples' thoughts, opinions or actions to rule my life. I oversaw my destiny and I could feel the pressure in my soul to not waste another second of it. Don't get me wrong, it was scary finding my footing again. It was really hard work.

I had never been alone before. I had to learn to accept every part of my soul…the good, the bad and the ugly. Once I changed my mindset and clearly set my intention on what I wanted in my life; everything changed and for the better.

It was just about two years after my divorce when I was blessed to find the love of my life. The one who embodied everything I wanted in a man. He was strong, confident, intellectual, respected, loyal, supportive and so much more. We both shared similar previous marriage experiences and knew that we were perfect for each other. From my experiences after marriage, I knew what I wanted and what I didn't want. The time alone afforded me a unique perspective on relationships and I thank God every day for him. I became a stepmother to his three beautiful boys and we embarked on blending our families together. This, of course, posed new different challenges that we needed to navigate, but at the end of the day we all love each other and enjoy the unique personalities each possess. When it came time to prep for my show, I was presented with nothing but loving support. Even if at the moment, he didn't quite understand my 'why' yet. I knew I couldn't have achieved the results I did without him by my side. When I had to sleep to work nightshift; he would cook my meals. When I said I was just too tired to work out; he stopped everything he was doing to give me a pep talk.

So, when I was up on stage, smiling from ear to ear, I couldn't have been prouder. The fifty pounds I shed was like a turbulent ocean that had stripped away years of sediment. There was no more doubt in my mind: only strength. No more self-sabotage; only momentum. There was no more self-loathing from mental abuse; only confidence. Confidence in who I was and who I had become: for my husband, my children and our family. I stopped comparing myself. I decided to surround myself with positivity. I figured out what made me happy and did just that.

Everything had changed.

It was like magic.

ABOUT EMILY BLAKE

Emily Blake was born in Warham, Massachusetts and as the daughter of a military family, she has lived all over. Longest residence being Griswold, CT where she graduated from Griswold Sr. High in 2000. After graduating high school, she started her first career at William W. Backus Hospital until December of 2018.

She is an avid fitness enthusiast, coffee lover, artist, blackbelt and proud mom of two boys Zachary and Austin as well as stepmom to three amazing boys Joshua, Adam and James. She is currently residing in Woodstown, New Jersey with her husband David and enjoys experiencing new things life has to offer.

Emily owns and operates Phoenix Pro Recovery as a Licensed Sports Massage therapist in Mullica Hill, New Jersey. You can locate her at www.phoenixprorecovery.com . Emily is currently a corrective exercise specialist and teaches through her online platform via Instagram @eblake526. She is certified in Graston technique, Functional cupping, Percussion Therapy and Facial Stretch Therapy. For those ready to recover quickly and reduce pain she is passionate about using her gifts along with her experiences to help everyone reach their full potential.

To connect with Emily:
Facebook: @emilyblakelmt
Instagram: @eblake526
Website: www.phoenixprorecovery.com

From Victim to Victor

Kim Pierre

I was born in 1969 in England Birmingham. I lived with my mother, father, older sister and younger brother. My earliest memories were that of atmosphere fights between mom and dad; not knowing what the atmosphere was going to be like from one day to the next. I believe this made me quite timid as a child. I hated loud noises as they would frighten me.

Subsequently, when I was around six years old my father left, leaving my mum financially struggling. She did her very best. However, it was tough since she did not have immediate family living close by as she had chosen to move away from the town that she had grown up in. Looking back, mom became very depressed at times and this made me sad as a child. I worried about my mom. Over time, mum made friends with the neighbours and this helped her as they would pop in for a cup of tea and us kids played together. We would go and see my Nan regularly; sometimes staying over. Mum's neighbours offered to help out with us kids while mum did a little cleaning job in the evening. One of mum's neighbour friend's husband offered to look after us while his wife and mom went out. This soon became most Saturday evenings. He said it would cheer mom up, but it was more about himself because he had other ideas of what "taking care of us" meant for me and my sister.

Mom having a little job, friends and evenings out with her friend made her happier. She started to enjoy life once again, however, this was certainly not the case for me and my sister as he sexually molested us for a year or so. The perpetrator told me that if we ever told anybody we would get into serious trouble and would not be believed. The abuse took place separately, but I knew because I could see the way she was around him. I never said a word to my mom or anyone else. Even at such a young age, I was worried I would not be believed and be the one in trouble. I felt worried that mom may not get over it. Even at this young age he had convinced me that telling was not an option, thus getting away with it.

Mom went on to meet a lovely man and he made her very happy. The abuse stopped as my mom's friend moved to a different area. We were saved from further abuse; divine intervention I would call it. I put the abuse to the back of my mind, however, I think this was the start of me identifying as a vulnerable victim at the age of seven years old. I believe the abuse added to my sensitivity. At the age of 12, on my way to school, I had a very odd feeling that something was not right. I went to stop for my friend as normal. When I got to her apartment, her mom said that she stayed with her other friend for the night and she was on her way back because she needed to pick something up for school. I said I would walk down to meet her. As I got in the elevator, a figure of what I thought was an old man through frosted glass walking as if stooped over got into the elevator with me. Then someone stopped the elevator and got in standing behind me. I didn't even look at the man, I just recall he had bright ginger hair. I remember very vividly; he started to breathe very heavily and was moving his hands. I was too afraid to turn around as I knew he was going to hurt me. I had a vision that he had a gun and he would shoot me. I then felt very calm. He proceeded to put a wire over my neck and started to pull tightly on the wire… strangling me. They say that your life can flash before you if you think you are about to die and my life started to flash before me as I was struggling to breathe. I kept seeing pictures of my life as a youngster. The elevator was now reaching the ground floor and I remember falling to the floor as I began to fight for my life. I don't know where I got my strength or overcome my fear as I started to fight by trying to shout, grab and kick him. He let go because I think this shocked him. I made as much noise as I could screaming at the top of my voice as I kept the elevator door open with my foot. I was not ready to die!

I think I might have passed out for a short period of time; seconds passed as I recall him running off and the caretaker of the apartments suddenly standing over me. At that point, I went into shock. The police were called and they wanted him for attempted murder, however, no one was ever arrested. I didn't receive any kind of counselling or support on how this might have affected me. When I look back, I know for sure that I felt I was definitely a vulnerable victim of life. I lost all interest in school and I did not want to go. When I did go, I just messed around. The apartment block was literally across from our school and of course my friend still lived there. This was a constant reminder of the incident each day. Consequently, I did not do very well at school and I left school with no qualifications. I do often wonder, had I received some support or counselling after the attack, would I have done better at school?

By this time mom had moved back to her hometown. She had met and married a man within six months. At that time, I did not like him and it was clear mom had rushed into it. She regretted marrying him. I could not handle the environment at home. I went to live with my friends and their mom. I was a young 16-year-old girl who had left home, no qualifications, no prospects, no guidance and I had no idea what the future held. I don't even think I cared at that point. I got a little cleaning job, had fun, went out and enjoyed myself. However, I always had an underlying feeling of unease about life.

Most likely due to the fact I had received no form of counselling of the past trauma. I just went along in life... never feeling at peace.

I went on to meet a man who was 20. I guess at 16 I thought I loved him, as 16-year-olds do. He wasn't an angel and had been in prison. However, when I met him, he was trying to turn his life around. He was a youth leader at the local church and although I knew he wasn't an angel he made me laugh. I thought he would look after me and I needed to feel loved. Looking back, he controlled me from day one. I lived with my friends and my sister. I spent most nights staying with him at his father's home. I had been with him for eight months and one morning we were woken by the police who arrested him. He remained in custody. Here I was lost, heartbroken, just seventeen years old, my boyfriend in prison and six weeks pregnant! I spent my pregnancy visiting him in prison and had the naïve notion that he would get out. Hoping we would have a great life when he got out. I was naïve; I was after all a child of 17 and totally lost in this world! I moved in with my partner's mother and went on to have my son. My son's father was released from prison and I thought everything would be fine. We found an apartment and I quickly remember thinking what have I done. I grew up quickly after having my son and I knew this was not the life I wanted with this man. He controlled me. I felt trapped, scared, confused and lonelier than I had ever felt in my whole life.

The seven years I spent with him felt like my own prison term. Over the seven years, his control became more and more frightening. There was no escaping him. I was physically, verbally, emotionally, sexually and mentally abused by this man. By now, I absolutely identified as a vulnerable victim and completely at his mercy. He would tell me how I would never amount to anything That I was stupid, not capable of anything or that my life would never be worthwhile and the best I could hope to achieve would be that of a toilet cleaner. Here I was, trying my very best to protect my son, to bring him up the best I could and he made my life hell. I remember thinking, when I get out of this, I will show him and the world exactly what I am capable of. I never stopped believing that, even in my darkest days. I felt totally trapped. I would leave and go to a different part of the country to a women's refuge; only for him to pay private detectives to find me. He would make promises to change, things would actually get worse and his behaviour to control just increased. The abuse in the early days would be that of punching, slapping and intimidation. That grew in its nature to quite traumatizing behaviour and several times I feared for my life.

I had a breakdown and I literally thought I was going to never gain my strength again. I would function around my son. Time alone was spent keeping a clean home and doing all I could to create normality for my son. I could sit for hours just staring into space; so afraid that I might not survive the hell I was in. Like any abusive relationship, there were times where things would be calm. However, that never lasted long and when things didn't go well in his life...I suffered the consequences. I was his stress ball that he was squeezing the life out of. The day I stopped identifying as a vulnerable victim, was the last day he ever laid his hands on me. I was at the sink in the kitchen washing up and I do not recall what started the incident. He was holding my hair and pushing my head in and out of the water. Each time I came up out of the water he had a knife to my throat. I looked at him and I looked up to the sky. I said *"This is enough I am **not** doing this any longer, just do what you want."* I meant it and he knew it. I just did not care anymore. I looked him in the eye and to this day I do not know what happened. I decided that day; I had to end this and take back my control. My behaviour seemed to shock him; as I truly meant what I said. He let go of my hair, put the knife down and walked out.

I took him to court, got an injunction out on him to prevent him from just coming and going from my home. I did this despite him always warning me that if I ever did, he would throw acid in my face to ensure that no other man would ever look at me. I could no longer live the life any longer. I guess it was stand up or die; I decided to fight back! I am not saying that it was easy and looking back it was a dangerous situation. He could have not responded in the way he did, but from that day forward he never laid another finger on me. I did still have a fear of his behaviour as he could be very unpredictable; I stood strong. Something that last day, of the last incident, changed my whole life.

For years, I always had a fear of creating a life. He would create so much anxiety in me. My confidence was too low to even try to create a life. I decided to take action. I was gaining more confidence. I enrolled at college and for the first time in my life, I felt normal. I was hopeful of my future and I was told I could do anything I put my mind to do. This gave me the confidence to find work and start to build a life of my own. I worked my way up with education, training and major determination to use my life experiences to help others. I set out to create a good income, to look after my son, to ensure he had a fulfilled mom who was capable of creating a good stable life for him, to educate him on how (despite the past) we could together overcome adversity and shine to become the amazing people we are today!

I was a senior care manager, a well-respected professional in my own right and I positively impacted so many lives through my career. I helped people with complex mental health and learning disabilities of duel needs. I also created jobs through my vision, ability and sheer determination to create and find a way when others couldn't see the vision. Which makes me so very proud. I knew I wanted to help people. It was a natural instinct in me, despite my background, I felt it was a calling of some sort.

My ex-partner continued to be unwell and had suffered a head injury during the time we were together. This went on to destroy his life by years of self-destruction causing chaos and destruction to many. After being wanted by the police for six years for murder and a whole host of despicable crimes, he was captured and hung himself in prison...a crack addict. I felt a great sense of freedom. I also felt a great sense of relief that he could no longer hurt other people. He was a very dangerous man and I was lucky to have escaped.

I know now my life happened *for* me and not *to* me. I can now be of service to others in need of healing from emotional pain. I have gratitude that I found the strength deep within me to overcome my past and live my best life ever. Guess what? You can too! You are more than you will ever know and stronger than you think. My advice would be if you are suffering in any form... get help. There is always a way. Do not stay thinking there is no way out. I am here to tell you that there is! My advice for you if you continue to suffer from past negative supressed emotions of trauma or emotions that no longer serve you; is to get help now! These can keep you stuck in the past and encroach on your present moment in time.

You are amazing, beautiful, strong and resilient. Seek help now to live your best life ever and go set the world on fire!

ABOUT KIM PIERRE

Kim lives in a small village on the outskirts of Birmingham, with her absolute rock (aka twin flame) Paul and her little fur baby Charly who is an adorable French bulldog.

Kim is an expert emotional healer. She helps people work through their emotions that can keep them stuck in life and preventing them from being the best version of themselves by holding them back. She works on releasing those suppressed emotions that they store deep down. These upiter ed emotions stop them from feeling free from their past. She guides them to release traumatic memories that no longer serve them. She walks with her clients each step of the way as they realize and understand the emotions. In doing this, it allows them to release emotions from their past and allows them to go on to do what their soul's purpose is in life.

Kim is a Jikiden Reiki practitioner. This originates from Japan and is authentic in its teaching to enable her to work through her energy to heal and promote well-being to those who receive it. She is also a safeguarding investigation manager for the largest social care housing association in the UK.

Her son (aka best friend) went on to make her the proudest mom in the world and he lives on the outskirts of Birmingham with his wife Steph and her three angels: Taylor 6, Jude 2 and Sienna 11 months old.

Kim counts herself blessed as her main aim and objective was that she could define her son not their past. He never ever disappoints from being the best son, husband and father any one could ever wish for. He works hard for his family, has ethics, morals and is the kindest person one could know. Kim often refers to him as the best thing that ever happened to her in her life and makes her very proud, every day.

You can connect with her at:

kim.possibleexperthealer@outlook.com
Facebook: Kim Pierre Expert Healer
and Instagram: Kim Pierre Expert Healer

Blazing my Own Trail

Dawn Broadwater

I was 16 years old when I married my high school boyfriend. I didn't have to get married as some girls do. I *wanted* to get married. I dreamed of the fairy tale life that awaited me. A life filled with love and laughter. A life that would be so very different from the life that I had lived up to that point.

As a child, I was sexually molested and bullied in school for several years. This only increased the feeling that something was dreadfully wrong with me. I was different. I felt that no one really liked me. I preferred keeping to myself and spending most of the time inside of my own head. After getting married, I felt safe and excited about each new day. Like every young newlywed, I had hopes and dreams of living happily ever after. I was still in high school. After school, I would come home to switch from student to wife. Cooking, cleaning and happily planning a future filled with fun. My life was about to go through a significant change. One I didn't see coming. It would forever change the course of my life. Two months after we were married, the honeymoon ended.

Being newly married...we didn't have a lot of money. For fun we would hang out with friends, party and play cards. Sometimes at our apartment and sometimes at our friends' homes. This one particular day, in November of 1977, while playing cards with several friends at their townhome; I made a comment to my new husband that he had thrown an incorrect card out. He disagreed. One of his friends agreed with me about the incorrect card and that he had taken a hand he shouldn't have. That one moment in time will be forever etched in my memory. Have you ever said something and almost immediately regretted saying it?

Everything happened so fast, but also felt like it was in slow motion. Cards were thrown, chairs knocked over and I knew in that moment my life would never be the same. I was pulled over the back of my chair and dragged by my hair through the parking lot to my car. I was thrown into the passenger seat and he went speeding down the road towards our apartment. He was punching me and screaming that when we got home, he was going to kill me. My only thought was to jump out of the car. I was terrified. I had never in my life heard of anyone being treated like this. My thoughts raced to my parents and that their only daughter was about to be murdered by a man they didn't want her to marry in the first place.

That was the beginning of nearly two decades of abuse. In two short months, all of my hopes and dreams of a happy life were destroyed.

Living in an abusive relationship was the most soul crushing thing I had ever been through. No matter how hard I tried to be perfect and do everything to make my husband happy; it was never good enough. Any moment could go from laughing and planning to have a nice day; to getting hit and holes being punched in doors or walls. The physical, mental, emotional, psychological and verbal abuse was delivered almost daily throughout those next two decades. Several times I packed up the kids and our belongings to move out while he was away from the house. He would always find us and woo me back with promises of change that things would be better. Sometimes it did change. It would be better for maybe a day or maybe even a week, but then we were right back in the middle of a war zone. Most of my days were spent isolated from the rest of the world. Friends I once had, were now driven away because they were a bad influence on me. My family, who lived just a couple miles away, had no idea what was happening in our lives. It was best that I didn't spend too much time with them for fear that they might find out the living hell their daughter and grandchildren were in. It was a horribly lonely time. I was depressed and scared every day. I never knew what was going to happen next. I managed my fear by self-medicating with anything I could get my hands on. Drugs and alcohol would take me away from the reality of my life; into a place that I could actually function. Until I couldn't anymore. It got to the point where I made a decision that it was time to end this way of life for me. I couldn't take another day. I knew that it would never end on its own. Sitting on the side of the bed, with the butt of a 12-gauge shotgun resting between my feet, I tried to muster up the courage to pull the trigger. I realized that he wouldn't be the one to find me. It would be the three little children in the next room who would. I couldn't do it. That was one of the lowest points in my life. The moment I knew that I would never get out of this hell.

When I turned 22 years old, something inside of me flipped. A switch was clicked on that made me want a better life for me and my kids. I quit all of the substance abuse and started thinking of how I could change my life. I had lived the past six years with everything going wrong. What did I have to lose? All of the mutual friends that my husband and I had up to that point, dropped their friendship with me. I wasn't one of them any longer. A 'good girl' that couldn't be trusted. Our lives continued on for the next couple of years. One day, I was reading the newspaper and there was an ad for a job at a local fast food store. I asked if I could go apply. He looked at me and laughed. He said to go ahead, but that I wouldn't get it. I thought he was probably right, but I had to try. If I was ever going to make a change in my life; it had to start right now. I went down to the place and filled out an application. I can still see the look on my husband's face when I pulled up in the gravel outside of our home and stepped out of the car holding my new uniform. The Earth had just tilted a little bit in my favor. That first job was a turning point for me. I was happy at work. Life at home might not have changed, but away from home I was a new person. My hopes and dreams were starting to come back, little by little. Soon after I started working, I found out I was going to have baby number four. I was so happy. Life was getting better. I had a job I loved. I was earning money and was going to have a baby. One thing that I remember, is that I was never physically abused while I was pregnant.

The marriage continued to deteriorate and after almost two decades; we divorced. I had grown much stronger being a working woman. I proved to myself that I could earn money and take care of myself. I knew that my life was only beginning. My past did not define my future and my future looked bright for the first time in my life. My kids and I could now build a life that was normal... whatever that was. We could be happy now. We could breathe. Not long after the end of my marriage, I received the words that no mother should ever hear. My 15-year old son had died while joy riding on the top of a freight train. My life went spiraling out of control. How could this happen? After everything we had been through. Everything we had gotten through. Everything we had lived through. Now, my son was gone. The total despair that engulfed me was too much. This was the darkest time of my entire life. Everything I had lived prior to this; didn't even compare to the agony I was in now. All hope was gone. For months, I just existed, not knowing what to do with my life. I was confused and unsure of myself. I didn't know how to live anymore. People didn't know how to behave around me. It was dark and very lonely.

A year after my son died; a new relationship was blossoming. I felt alive again. I felt hopeful of having a future that was filled with love and laughter. After only dating for two months, we were married. I knew that this man was going to give me all of the love I had so desperately wanted; or so I thought. Almost immediately after we were married; he started cheating on me. I was devastated. How could I have been so wrong? I wanted this marriage to work. I had put so much hope in it bringing the happiness I had longed for. I was pregnant and the following summer we welcomed our new little girl. This marriage was not physically abusive, but the mental and psychological abuse was once again crushing. I was still in a very depressed state after losing my son and this just piled on top. It was too much. In the spring of 1999, just two days after Mother's Day, I stood at the kitchen counter and took an entire bottle of my husband's pain pills. It was the end of a life that I felt I should never have lived. It wasn't just the cheating husband I was now married to. It was the death of my son.

It was the abuse of my first marriage. It was the bullying combined with sexual abuse of my childhood. It was asking for help and not getting any. It was trying to figure everything out on my own and failing miserably. It was just one more thing on a growing pile of 'one more thing' until I just couldn't bring myself to go on for another day. Years of trying to please everyone else. Trying to make them like me or love me. It had dissolved who I really was. I was willing to become whoever I needed to be for people to want me in their life. I would do almost anything for people to like me or love me. Pretty soon, I didn't even know who I was anymore.

As you may have guessed, I lived through that night. I was found lying on a bike trail in the middle of the night; by a man that I honestly feel was an angel. He saved my life. I wish I could say that my life changed into a wonderful and happy existence after that; but that didn't happen. The marriage eventually ended and with that I lost literally everything I had. My home. My belongings. My business. Everything. Everything, except my life. I still had my life. After several years with just myself and my kids to worry about; I felt my life becoming happy. I started to wonder what I wanted my life to be like. Where I wanted my life to be. In one of my 'day-dreaming' moments, I called my cousin who lived in Oregon. I asked her if I moved up to Oregon; would she let me and my now 8-year-old daughter stay with her until I found a job with a new home? She said yes.

I was scared and elated at the same time. *Could I do this? Could I pack up my life and my little girl? Could I move away from the only home I had ever known? Could I leave my family, my friends and my job to go start a new life in Oregon?* All the questions came firing at me. *What if it doesn't work? What if I fail? What if I can't find a job? What if I lose everything?* The most important question I asked myself was: *What if it DID work?* After that phone call to my cousin, I gave my employer a three-month notice. In June 2006, I left everything behind and moved to Oregon. Terrified I was making a wrong choice and worried I had just done the worst possible thing. I drove that moving truck out of Sacramento County and onto Interstate 5 heading north to my new life.

It has been almost 14 years since that June day and I have never regretted it for a single minute. I have learned to love myself and my life. I have forgiven myself for not making the best choices over the past 50+ years. I am letting myself have the happy life I dreamed of, but never really thought was possible. During these past 14 years, I have welcomed all of my grown children and their children to Oregon. They have started new lives for themselves. I adopted my oldest granddaughter; who is keeping me young. I met and married the soul mate I had dreamed of; ever since I was a little girl. I never knew how good love could feel and how life changing it is to be unconditionally loved for whom you are. I moved out to my sweetheart's home in the country. I work in my garden. I watch the raising of pigs, cows and horses that roam around on the property.

If you would have asked me 40 years ago, if I ever thought that I would be living the life I live now...I would have told you no. Looking back at my life, there is no way anyone would have thought that I would be where I am today. From a battered mom who lived on welfare and was self-medicated just to escape the nightmare reality of her life; to the successful entrepreneur who lives every day with laughter and excitement for what's next.

I am here to tell you that if I can do it; you can do it.

Never give up! Your best life is waiting!

ABOUT DAWN BROADWATER

Dawn Broadwater was born in France and raised in Orangevale, California. She is the mom of four beautiful daughters who have blessed her with nine grandchildren and one great grandchild. She resides in the Pacific Northwest with her husband Richard and together they are raising Dawn's oldest granddaughter. Dawn enjoys gardening in her 4000 square foot garden and Harley rides with Richard enjoying the countryside around their property in Dallas, Oregon.

Dawn is the founder and coach of Dawn Broadwater Coaching and is passionate about living her purpose. Her purpose is to use her positive enthusiasm to support and inspire women to absolutely believe in themselves along with the power they possess.

To connect with Dawn, visit Facebook: @dawnbroadwater

Standing in Truth and Walking in Balance

Alicia Thorp

Have you ever looked at someone and found yourself pre-judging them? Did you ever stop to consider what circumstances they might have went through that made them the person they are today? Being judged by strangers for using food stamps and state assistance after an extreme and long divorce process changed the course of my life forever. It challenged me in ways I never expected. It drove me to where I am today. It forced me to live in balance and stand in my truth. It made me start living in alignment. This is my story of learning to live in balance by following my intuition and living confidently in my truth. Living in truth, no matter what the whispers were behind my back of people judging me.

Starting again, after my divorce, was a challenge. A challenge I never thought I would personally have to deal with. I didn't picture my life with traumatic events, court appearances or clouded with uncertainty. Needless to say, here I was facing all of that as a newly single mom with no full-time income. I was just trying to make ends meet. I found myself standing in more lines trying to get the assistance I needed; rather than job interviews. I saw myself being judged by others. Others, who had no idea what my truth was or what I was going through. It was that judgment coupled with harsh reality that made me even more determined to find my balance and get my personal power back. I needed to find consistency, stability and structure. It wasn't easy, but I knew it was possible. I wasn't sure how at the time, but I had that gut feeling that I was meant for more. I would move forward with my head held high and with dignity. I did this even as I was living with minimal income and state assistance. Just because I had a pretty crappy situation to deal with in that moment, didn't mean that I had to be stuck there. I could still move forward. It was okay for me to take time to notice where I was. It was okay to have a sense of gratitude for my life in order to rise up every single day, stronger and with more passion in my heart than the day before. I was not full of myself for standing with my head held high as a survivor of my life. I was choosing to not be a victim. I began to realize that showing vulnerability doesn't mean you are weak. Instead, it means you are aware. With this awareness, I learned to be okay taking my time when making decisions. I learned it was okay to say no to opportunities that did not feel good to me.

If I was going to have the job I wanted, the life I wanted, maybe even another loving relationship...I had to start living in alignment with strength. I had to learn to trust myself and love myself again.

I slowly began to find my footing. I was no longer accepting mediocracy. I was no longer willing to be surrounded with people or situations that made me feel uncomfortable. As I began to accept my life truth; I began to grow in confidence. I was pulled away from jobs that didn't serve me, from friends that were no longer adding positive value and from environments that were not in my best interest. I was putting down the 'people pleasing' vibes and beginning to use manifestation instead. This was particularly important when it came to the relationships I had in my life. They didn't just affect me, but also my young child during this time. I found myself joining business networking groups and being surrounded with more like-minded people. These people understood what it was like to deal with a traumatic situation and not live in the negative. These friends found the strength to build the life of their dreams. I used manifestation skills to find my current husband. Right down to very specific details. I noticed that my life could be the way I choose. I learned the power of visualization. I began to visualize and believe my visions as truth; before they even happened. I started to find my power. My magic. I loved the feeling of living in balance and realized that I did not have to live less than anyone else. The truth of my life was determined by ME, not anyone else. It is okay to be specific about my life. Contrary to popular belief, it is not snobby. It is all about alignment.

I explored avenues such as yoga and wellness. A path which led me to find meditation and mindfulness. I implemented all of these physical practices into my life. Using these new techniques, it helped me to see my obstacles as speed bumps; not road blocks. These obstacles were not going to stop me from living the life I wanted, but they were giving me the chance to slow down before moving forward. Through this time, I began using more gratitude in my life. This slowly became my 'go to' strategy whenever negative thoughts from the past would creep in and I needed to change my mindset. I was able to consciously find balance in life; no matter how busy life seemed to be. Finding balance does not mean I didn't ever think negatively or that I wasn't hard on myself at times. Instead, it meant I was able to notice my thoughts, acknowledge them, adjust them if needed, be grateful for them and then move forward in a more peaceful state of mind. I was living in a conscious state of awareness. Let me tell you, that is a beautiful way to live. Balance became my vision in life. It became my passion. It's what I was meant to share to individuals who were in similar situations as me.

In conversation, you would rarely hear me say that I was a victim of domestic violence in my earlier years. It's not that I ignore that part of my life, I just am consciously aware that I am not in that phase of my life any longer. It is more important to be in the present moment. I choose to live my current life with love and a grateful heart versus dwelling on the past or on situations that I have moved on from. I am able to see the challenges, bring in the gratitude, see the bigger picture and live in balance. If I did not make the choice to live consciously, I would be stuck in my head with past thoughts and even past emotions. I would be overrun with overwhelm, anxiety, PTSD and tears. I would be spiraling down the dark hole that was my life. I remind myself, without the dark and stormy road, the sun and the rainbows would not have shown up in my life. I see my blessings daily and it brings me back to that conscious state of awareness, balance and peace.

I wasn't given this life so I could play small and hide. Life had shown me some dark times as a magical challenge to my soul. One that made me show up more and to prove to myself how strong I really am. I love to share my passion of living in alignment, living with gratitude and living a balanced life through the ups and downs. I am now able to run a mindset business, host yoga classes, throw vision board parties, run online courses, do group coaching, mentor and inspire others through breathing techniques all while raising kids, having a family, working a 9-5 and being involved in community events. In less than one year, I became a best-selling author (twice), was published in multiple magazines, featured in online empowerment summits and had opportunities to speak in front of amazing groups of individuals who wanted to hear my message of balance and productivity! My biggest message to you...*you can do it too!* Peace and balance can be mastered when the work you do is fulfilling and in alignment with what feels good. I am able to help others master this combination in their busy lives so they can increase their peace and productivity too.

Here are two major techniques that I invite you to use for yourself. I have found these to be pivotal in my own life journey in finding balance and peace. Finding a morning routine was how it all began for me. I knew I needed to take some time for me before I was giving to everyone around me. Sound familiar? Something like the phrase, 'you can't pour from an empty cup'?

First, I started with some mediation practices and taking at least 20 minutes to myself in the morning. So many times, we are pulled into the world and the events going on around us, without even realizing it. Social media, television and radio are all pulling our minds elsewhere. Even before we have started the day. If this sounds like you, how could you change your morning routine? I bet you would be able to find more peace and balance in your day through some small changes. Consciously having the vision of balance in my life allows me to do it all without losing my way or my direction. This lifestyle allows me to smile more, love more, laugh more and be overall happier throughout each moment. Being a positive person is not something you can just wake up and be. It takes intention. Balance, positivity and peace is a mindset. Using your thoughts to change your perspective and to see solutions in your life rather than problems; plays a big role.

Second, how does it sound to take ten minutes to write down all the blessings you have and show gratitude for your life each morning? Would you need more time or would you think that is too much time? I challenge you to try this every day for one single week. I can guarantee by the end of the week those ten minutes will fly by and you will have so many more things to write down that you are appreciative of.

Your life circumstances do not have to define you. Instead, they can change you and make you see things in a different way. The negative actions of others are a reflection of who they are; not you. You can take your situations and turn them around to create the most magical life that you choose.

If you want to be a stay at home mom...do it!

If you want to be the CEO of your own business…do it!

If you want to travel to see the world…do it!

The only person stopping you is *YOU!*

Which also means, the only person that can create the life of their dreams is *YOU!*

Begin where you are. Life is not meant to be lived focusing on regret or the bad times from your past. No, it is meant to be celebrated.

Bring in your balance, gratitude and peace.

Watch your life take off.

Never forget, *YOU* are magic!

ABOUT ALICIA THORP

Alicia Thorp is a Holistic Mindset Mentor, Author and Speaker who guides busy women to create a balanced lifestyle so they can achieve massive transformation. Alicia's mentoring will leave you feeling empowered to live in your truth while finding balance in it all. Alicia is a spiritual entrepreneur with a nurturing and heart-centered soul and is passionate about helping others.

Alicia is a busy mom, wife, coffee lover, yoga instructor and nature lover.

You can connect with Alicia on the web at www.aliciathorp.com or connect with her on social media.

Finding Serendipity

Anne Marie Moorer

The water moved and despite the cold, it gave me comfort. Listening to the sound of the wind blowing through the barren forest, I heard a squeal from a branch in its final efforts to fight the wind and stay on the tree. I looked up to find it. Eventually, another gust blew allowing me to track the sound...just in time to witness the branch surrendering to its fate and finally letting go. As I sat there, alone in the woods, in my familiar spot over the past year...a tear spilled down my cheek. Surrender and letting go seemed to be a common theme for me over the past few years. This past year, whenever I felt the shadows creeping in, I would retreat to this place: my little sanctuary in the woods. It offered me space to be quiet with my thoughts, to be still without interruption, remember my training while bearing witness to nature's greatest lessons of seasons, cycles and the beauty within them. Nature reminds us that no matter how dark the night, the sun will rise again. No matter how long or hard the winter, spring will come and with it will bring new life, new beauty, new opportunities and new magic.

On this particular day in the forest, I reflected on my life, my shadows and the darkness they bring. The shadows I refer to is a term I believe everyone can relate. I chose to label my times of challenge and struggle, not for drama or to make light of them, but for what they were. Darkness. *'Darkness'* is a powerful word that can contain many things: fear, trauma, anger, heartbreak, abuse, disappointment, rejection, failure, etc. Shadows bring darkness. These words can describe it poetically without divulging the details. I can tell you that these times in my life were difficult and required hard work to get through. Details do not matter in this story, though mine may differ from yours, darkness is relative.

My first experience with my *'shadows'* began in my early teens. These can be awkward times for many: finding your place, trying on different faces to see where you fit or don't fit. Since I was young, I knew I was different and my school years certainly confirmed that! I felt things very deeply and I struggled...I guess you could say I had it harder than some, but better than others. In looking back on my life, this was the first time I can recall that I followed that feeling, that voice within me to create something different for my life. That inner knowing pushed me to take a job at 14, which gave me a taste of independence through earning my own money. I changed the course of my studies to enter into the Cosmetology program in high school. I didn't have the foresight to know how that would change my life; I just knew that it was the right decision for me at that time.

The next several years were exciting! After graduation, I secured a job in a salon and I was doing what I loved. I was helping people feel better about themselves; which made me happy. I felt connected. I was creative in my craft and quickly built a clientele. I was in the 'flow'. I was connected spiritually, studying energy and different belief systems. I was curious. This curiosity led me to travel and have different experiences. It also led me to begin college part time to earn a degree in marketing and management for small business. I was still working. I was grateful. I was able to ride the ebbs and flows of life without much resistance. It was *serendipitous!* For many years, every corner I turned led me straight to *serendipity.*

After I finished my degree, my parents urged me to explore a more stable career. One that offered benefits and a pension. I wasn't certain it was what I should do. After combining logic with the respect for my parents, I agreed to the new journey. I secured a position that offered all of these perks, while maintaining my job in the salon on nights and weekends. I embarked on a new chapter. After a few years, the shadows returned. I was tired. Working 65-hour weeks and two jobs was taking its toll. It certainly did not allow much creative time for me. I was spiritually disconnected. I was discontent with my personal life and my day job brought me no pleasure or sense of purpose. Once again, that feeling within me stirred and that voice urged me to change course. This time it was not just a feeling stirring within me, but a child. I was 26 and going to become a single mother. To say that *Fear* didn't appear in his suit of grandeur at this point would be a lie. He was there. However, I was pleasantly surprised to see just behind him came his adversaries *Hope, Determination* and *Love*. Despite circumstances, I loved this little life in me so much that I knew I would do whatever it took to take care of us. I was determined and had a new purpose.

A few weeks after discovering I was with child; I was presented with an opportunity to purchase an existing salon. I believe, had the circumstances been any different, the opportunity would not have been revealed to me or I might have chosen differently. That salon was a lifeline to me and I grabbed it. To others it seemed completely illogical, to give up the "security" position with a child on the way, but to me it was the only decision to be made. The fire in me returned and at five months pregnant, I opened my first salon. I followed my intuition, trusted that inner voice and had faith in the Universe. I was immediately surrounded by beautiful angels on this earth who appeared in various forms to help me succeed. I will not say it was all easy. There were many times that I was humbled. Despite those things, I was back in the flow of life and back in the light. The next few years were happy and exciting! I was blessed with a beautiful little boy; my business was successful and I expanded our little family through marriage and a second child. I eventually closed the salon and went to work for someone in order to spend more time at home with my children. This particular time period was a flurry of diapers, toddlers, play dates, pets and a new home. Serendipity had visited me in many forms throughout those years. Eventually, the shadows began to appear around the edges of my life and before I knew it, hello Darkness, my old friend.

It was during this time that I got caught up in the details. I allowed myself to be consumed by them. Personally, and professionally, I was not fulfilled. My marriage was ending. It was dark. I suffered. I grasped to a vision of how I thought things should be rather than accepting them for what they were. I was no longer in touch with myself. I was no longer certain of my purpose. I was resisting my inner voice and going against what I knew was best for me. Within a three year span I had a hysterectomy, a wrist surgery and ended up in the hospital with a terrible case of pneumonia which took months to recover from. That was the final straw.

I knew things had to change radically or I would stay in the shadows forever. Once again, I went within to search for the answers only I could find. That familiar feeling would not cease and that inner voice screamed, *"It is time!"*. I knew that if I were to have happiness in my life, it was up to me to create it. I toyed with looking for spaces for another salon, but I needed a name. Quite loudly, I was given one. I quickly searched the meaning and the definition read *"look for something and find something more suited to your needs"*. Perfect! There could be no other name. That day, at my computer, I did not hesitate. I did not over think it. My fingers moved swiftly over the keyboard and I created an LLC. Serendipity Salon was conceived. Things progressed rapidly once that decision was made. The perfect space became available. Once again, I was surrounded by earth angels to support me and help me erect this beautiful space to create my happiness. The next few months were a blur. I know I was being guided by a higher power. The Blessings bestowed on me in such a short time were unexplainable otherwise. I created the LLC in March and Serendipity Salon opened its' doors for the first time in November of that same year. The list of angels who appeared to help me is long: employees, friends, family, architects, plumbers, electricians and more. I can never express the gratitude that I will forever hold for these people, my angels.

The next several years were not without new challenges, however, it was a wonderful time of growth, reacquainting with myself, my life and my purpose. As part of my own healing, I began practicing yoga. I quickly realized the benefits of the practice, not only for my body, but for my mind. My curiosity led me to enroll in teacher training. I learned how to better care for my mind, body and spirit. I became a certified 200hr yoga instructor. I discovered that I loved teaching and sharing this ancient practice to help others. That decision brought more angels to me. Since I was young, I have always been called to the metaphysical realm: intuition, magic, energy and the roles they play in our lives. Most of my experience was solitaire. Through yoga, a community of like-minded individuals were revealed to me. It provided space for me to share, learn and grow in my gifts. I was called to the art of healing and became a Reiki II practitioner. I embraced my intuition and devotionally returned to the studies of energy, magic and manifestation. I found amazing teachers, mentors and friends who have forever changed the course of my life. I discovered the magic within me and openly began to share with my friends, family and clients. I accepted my intuition as a gift and a tool that can help to guide others through their own journey. I have always loved serving and helping people. Looking back, throughout my life, it has always been my connection with people that has lit my soul on fire. What could be better than sharing all of this with others? This is me. This is my purpose. New love entered my life along with new experiences and wonderful *serendipity*.

It was a wonderful time and as seasons always change; so does life. Shadows began to creep in once again. This darkness brought loss, not once, but several times. All in different forms and in less than two years. Looking back, only now can I recognize where I lost my way and where

I strayed from my purpose. I allowed the needs of others to over shadow my own. I gave up my daily practices unbeknownst to me, to become what I thought others needed me to be. I did not value myself. I lost my power and my magic. It was a hard year for me.

As the new year was quickly approaching, I wanted desperately to end the year and start new. I spent a lot of time alone, doing the work, recommitting to my daily practices, to finding my magic and my way. I was tired. That branch, surrendering to its fate in my sanctuary in the woods, prompted me to go over my life with an objectivity I hadn't had in a few years. I began to see the gifts I had been offered this past year, despite heartache and yet, because of it. I had committed to healing me. I completed my 500hr yoga training, traveled to the West, fell in love with mountains, hiking and began returning to myself. I recognized patterns in myself, my life and the lessons they represented. I recognized where in my life I continually gave my power away. I began to accept myself and recommit to my daily practices that ground me. I realized that every time I have strayed from my practice and my purpose...the shadows appear to remind me. It is when I ignore them, darkness arrives.

Hope and *Determination* showed up again assuring me that 2020 would be a better year yet! It began with old friends and new opportunities. I made the decision that day in the woods to stop getting caught up in the details of the darkness within my shadows. I decided to focus instead on creating. To find my spark and *serendipity*, once again. Once that decision was made, in true fashion, things began happening very quickly. Multiple opportunities arose to share my gifts, to help others create and manifest their best lives through energy work, teaching, tarot and yoga. I was contacted by one of those angels I met, so many years ago, in my first yoga training. She asked me to reach out to a publisher to tell my story. So, here I am, sharing with you the lessons I've learned.

Every time I have been forced to pause and to sit in the dark; there were lessons for me. Those lessons always reveal that I am resisting some part of my true self. I was playing small. I was attached to an idea, belief or outcome that I wanted to be true; instead of trusting what is to be. I've realized that every time I have surrendered and let go of those attachments, I was presented with new opportunities, new levels of consciousness and wonderful *serendipity*. I have found when you commit to self-reflection, self-development, work on improving yourself and your relationship with others...there is no option, but to grow. I have helped many on their path and look forward to continuing to do so. I have also been the one in need of help to see clearly. I have recognized, that despite our differences, we are the same. Through it all, *Hope* and *Determination* continue to take my hand and show me the way. Through a long winding journey of stumbles and falls, I have found my purpose. I am a healer. Serving others and helping them find their beauty in this world has been my purpose for the past three decades.

As far as finding *serendipity,* I believe it's always around the next corner if you are willing to step out of your shadows and into your light. Trust that what is meant for you will be. It has been said that those that don't believe in magic, will never find it. The same is true for *serendipity.* If you surrender and let go; you may find that instead of what you were searching for...you will find something more suited to your needs. On that day, in the woods, it all came together for me. I went there to grieve and to heal, but instead I was shown the beauty and light that shone through the many cracks of seemingly imperfections in my life. That is *serendipity* my friends... That is *magic.*

ABOUT ANNE MARIE MOORER

Anne Marie is a proud Mom to two beautiful young men, 500 hr. RYT yoga instructor, Reiki ll practioner, mystic, tarot reader, intuitive, healer and perpetual student of life.

Anne Marie is a stylist and owner of Serendipity Salon in her hometown of West Deptford, New Jersey. She is passionate and committed to sharing her gifts and 30 years of experience to help others recognize their outer and inner beauty.

In her spare time, she enjoys practicing yoga, hiking, traveling and spending time with family and friends.

You can connect with her on Facebook:
https://www.facebook.com/annemarie.moorer

via email: TheMagickofSerendipity@gmail.com

Magic of Flight

Molly Peebles

Vernon opened the passenger door to the single engine Cessna 152 and climbed out. He poked his head back in and looked straight at me smiling, *"Hey Molly...you've got this!"* With that, he closed the door. I watched my pilot instructor walk away and head to the control tower.

For a few moments, I felt like I was six years old on my first day of kindergarten watching my mom walk away. Could I do this without my instructor? Would I remember everything to successfully fly solo in this plane? There would be no back-up. No one to ask if I questioned something. It would be up to me. You can't just pull off to the side of the road up there! Taking off means commitment to the finish. Could I do it?

That feeling of smallness and self-doubt quickly left, replaced by my out-loud pep-talk, *"Molly, you trained for this, you've taken off and landed a hundred times. You know how to do this. YOU KNOW HOW TO DO THIS!"*

I radioed the tower my request to conduct my solo flight on 36L and would be staying in the flight pattern. After receiving my instructions, I taxied to the run-up area and completed my pre-takeoff checklist.

When you receive the clearance for takeoff, you have to go. There could be planes in line to land and you have to get out of the way. There is no time to second-guess yourself. Once you taxi to the runway and hear, *"Cleared for takeoff"*, it's 'GO' time.

"Molly, are you going to do this? Or not?", came the voice in my head. *"Paine Tower, Cesna 714TangoDelta at Alpha 5 ready for solo flight touch-and-go's"*, I heard myself say.

"Four TangoDelta, you are cleared for take-off".

I gently pushed in the throttle and taxied onto the runway into position. It was 'GO' time. No looking back. Now the throttle went in all the way. I watched my instruments and waited for my airspeed to rise...then slowly pulled back the yoke...wheels up...airborne...flaps up to 20 degrees...then 10...all the way up. At 1000 feet, I pitched the nose down to level off and banked left to begin the landing pattern.

Three months earlier, I had been on Whidbey Island attending a Shamanic workshop. In the middle of a divorce, I had some processing left to do. It was a retreat that brought up all my "stuff". Instead of the healing and comfort I had been hoping for; I left depressed and confused. As I was driving on the freeway towards home, a loud voice within said, *"Molly, you would feel so much better if you could have a flight in a small plane."* Really?? I had seen a grass field runway on my drive up and sure enough, there was the turnoff. I drove to the office and quickly saw that it was closed. Really?? I burst into tears and began my rant to the Universe which went something like, *"I went to this retreat...now I feel worse...trying to follow Divine Guidance...and now it's closed...what do you want from me??...I just want my life to count...just want to make a difference in the world and be of service...you're not helping me...you brought me here and it's closed?! What the heck does that mean?!"* For an hour, I sobbed and journaled, letting out pent up thoughts and emotions. After gathering myself together, I got back on the road and headed south. A half hour later I noticed a sign for Paine Field. An airport?? I took the exit and followed the signs to Regal Air, an FBO and flight school for general aviation pilots and "wanna-be's". The lobby was spacious and filled with artwork of planes spanning the eras. At the front desk I inquired about how to get a flight in a small plane. They had flight instructors who could take me on a demo flight, but I would have to wait two hours. I had children at home and couldn't wait. I was sent home with a folder full of information on what makes planes fly and the steps to getting a pilot's license. I spent the week pouring over the information. I found myself both fascinated and excited.

The following weekend, I was back on the Island for another retreat. This time I left feeling empowered. This would be my day to fly. It was a bright blue-sky day and I was ready. I made my way back to Regal Air and this time my wait would be 15 minutes. The flight instructor greeted me and we walked out to the aircraft. After our pre-flight check, I found myself sitting in the pilot's seat, headset on and turning the key to start the engine. The loud drone of the propeller vibrated the plane. The instructor piloted us to the runway, explaining everything along the way and then we took off! We got up to 3000 feet and headed over Puget Sound. The view was astounding! The instructor told me to take the yoke and turn it to the left. We immediately started a shallow bank. Encouragingly, he instructed me to be more assertive and take the bank steeper. I was to watch the attitude indicator and shoot for a 30-degree steep bank turn. My stomach lightened and clenched from the G-forces! I gently pulled out of it and then took the steep turn to the right. I couldn't believe I was doing this! I never would have thought that flying a plane was something I could do. But here I was, flying! The instructor told me what we would be doing to land the plane and that he would talk me through it. His hands would also be on the controls, but as back-up. I was the pilot-in-command. I pitched the yoke downward to descend and he brought back the throttle to lower our airspeed. I lined up the nose of the plane with the lines on the runway, which got bigger as we got closer. When instructed, I raised the nose...pause...the back wheels touched down followed by the front wheel. We taxied off the runway and back to Regal Air. Elation and utter excitement filled me. I had just flown a plane! I never dreamed of doing such a thing!

As I drove home that evening, I decided that by the time I turned 40—seven years from then—I wanted to learn to fly a plane. I had three young children at home and I was a single parent. Life was busy. By the time I got home, I realized that if I was putting this off for seven years because I thought eventually there would be a more convenient time, I was kidding myself. I would always be busy! So why wait? If I wanted to do this, I should go for it and do it now. No excuses. Running in the house, I called Regal Air and signed up for Ground School. Flight lessons would begin two weeks later.

I was now on the downwind, settling into my seat and the freedom of flying solo. To my left was the beautiful water of Puget Sound. The tiny white dots of boats were scattered on the royal blue water below. Being in the air and seeing the world from the birds-eye view was exhilarating. Air traffic control radioed that a 747 heavy was incoming and I would need to leave the landing pattern. I chose to head out over the water to circle while I waited for clearance to return. It was an unexpected, yet welcomed detour that allowed me more time to take in the magic of flight. I could soak in this extraordinary moment and accomplishment in my life. Once back in the landing pattern, I successfully completed my solo flight. Take-off...land...then full-throttle to take off again. Do that three times and you receive your instructor's written endorsement that you are now a Student Pilot, eligible to rent and fly a plane (with restrictions). The Student Pilot status allows the student to practice skill maneuvers on their own between lessons.

Each time I went to the airport to practice, I was met with a choice. I would go out to the plane, thinking about the maneuvers I needed to practice: slow flight, stalls, turns-around-a-point, steep bank turns, short field take-offs and landings. These skills would need to be practiced and perfected in preparation for the FAA check ride. It would be the final test to becoming a certified pilot. Anticipating practicing these skills was both exciting and frightening! That voice would always greet me, "*Molly, are you going to do it? Or not? Are you going to feel the fear and do it anyway? Or are you going to turn around and go home?*" The choice was always clear to me. Climbing into that left front seat and being pilot-in-command was the thing to do. I would most certainly feel the fear and question my readiness each time. *Can I do this? Will I remember?* I gave myself permission to re-evaluate my confidence level once in the sky, but I had to get in the sky. Every time I said, "yes", took that 714TD into the air for a couple of hours and land again; I would hop out of the plane 10 feet taller. Every flight built my confidence in my flying abilities, confidence in myself and expanded what I thought was possible!

On October 23, 2001, I passed my FAA check ride and became a pilot.

It was right after 9/11 and the whole aviation industry was depressed. There was great angst and uncertainty if general aviation pilots like myself would be able to fly unrestricted as we had before. So many people were afraid to fly at that time. I, however, was on top of the world. I was a pilot! I could FLY!! The process of learning to fly a plane had transformed me. It had stretched me and challenged me. I had to rise to a new level! I had to expand what I thought was possible and I proved to myself that I was capable of far more than I ever thought! Out of the tragedy of 9/11 came an idea…a way for pilots to take back our beloved skies and use aviation to bring healing to people across our nation and beyond. I had a vision of pilots across the country flying in honor of the fallen and in tribute to the gift of flight.

On January 1, 2002, I awoke to that voice in my head again, *"Molly, are you going to do it or not? Flight Across America! Are you going to do it?? Or not??"* My first thought was: sure, I'd look into it. A national aviation event would take time—years—to put together. Sure, I would think about it. The next day, I spoke with a dear friend and told her about my idea. *"Molly"*, she said, *"you have to do it at the one-year anniversary!"* Impossible, I thought, that is only nine months away! Later that day, I went to the airport to fly with my instrument instructor. I told Rob I was so excited about this idea I had and I couldn't concentrate on flying until I told him about it. *"Molly"*, he said, *"you have to do it at the one-year anniversary!"*

Indeed. From August 11 to September 11, 2002, more than 3,000 planes registered flights as part of the *"Flight Across America"*. Opening ceremonies were held at Paine Field in Everett, WA and closing ceremonies were held on board the U.S.S. Intrepid Air & Space Museum aircraft carrier in New York City. A single-file processional flight of pilots representing every state and Puerto Rico flew down the Hudson River corridor, past the Statue of Liberty and Ground Zero.

In that very first demo flight, I experienced the magic of flight. The miracle of becoming airborne and seeing the world from an expanded viewpoint. The process of learning to fly, the opportunities to choose "yes" in the face of fear or doubt...expanded my understanding of myself and my capabilities. I discovered that truly, the only limits we have are the ones we place on ourselves.

The invitation is to set ourselves free.

Spread your wings...feel the magic...and take flight.

ABOUT MOLLY PEEBLES

Molly Peebles has been using life experiences as an intentional path for self-discovery for decades. An adventurous spirit, she learned to fly a plane, climbed mountains in Peru, hiked in the Amazon, traveled around the globe and now participates in Spartan Obstacle Races. She discovered the path to physical fitness to be a personal and spiritual growth journey that taught her resilience, grit, and how to overcome obstacles in life or on the course.

Molly is a #1 International Best-Selling Author, Inspirational Speaker and Life Reinvention Coach. Using the experience of flying as a metaphor, she teaches and inspires her audience and shows them how to become pilot-in-command of their own life. She also combines elements of the Medicine Wheel, Shamanic worldview, whole-body fitness and well-being to lead transformational programs and adventure retreats.

She has a great love of the outdoors. When she's not speaking or teaching, you will find her hiking, snowshoeing and training for her next obstacle race or mountain summit. Molly has three adult children and lives with her wife Suzan in Bothell, WA.

To connect with Molly, visit
www.mollypeebles.com
Facebook: @mollypeebles

My Two Seasons

Janet Brent

Throughout my life, I have tried my best to follow my intuition. I always felt there was something *more* for me. More than a job. More than a paycheck. When the whispers of my heart led me, I listened. I listened when it told me to quit my job, quit a toxic relationship, move to the Philippines to get in touch with my cultural roots and start a freelance business. It may have taken me years to find the courage to do so, but when I finally did…there was no turning back.

My soul's calling started small and nondescript at first. As the years went on, it shifted into ways that felt more specific, more purpose-driven and far more urgent to follow. I call these chapters of my life: my two seasons. Each gave me a new layer to learn from. A new layer to get past. A new layer to conquer. From manifestation and following my intuition; I created my very own rags to riches success story.

The First Season: Eat Pray Love

Being a child of words and books; they have been anthems of my life that I wrapped around me like a cozy scarf around my neck, a signature to my clothing style. Not essential, but an accessory to express myself. That's what books felt like. They were a mixtape to my life.

I stumbled upon Eat, Pray, Love during the rocky point of my toxic relationship. It inspired many women to break-up from lackluster relationships and pursue their dreams. Myself included. It inspired my spiritual awakening, already trickling in with my newfound meditation practice.

When the voice inside told me to move to the Philippines, get in touch with my cultural roots and start my freelance design business...I thought it was crazy. Getting into the minimalist and digital nomad movement through various blogs online made it feel less so. My dreams turned into reality when I bought a one-way ticket to India, where I committed to a volunteer group and then bought a one-way ticket to the Philippines with no set plans. I sold all my stuff and off I went with less than $1,000 to my name.

Thus, began my magical year of living with less. Although I wanted it to be a true gap year, my first development led me to a headhunter job–hired on the spot. It felt too good to be true and it probably was. The man was willing to train me from scratch in the recruiting industry, but a few red flags made me intuitively feel this wasn't what I was supposed to do.

"Universe, give me a sign. If there's something better out there for me, I'll take it!"

With no set plans, I was open to the open-ended freedom. That very next day, a Buddhist monastery retreat opportunity fell into my lap when I wasn't looking. It was to be held in two different monasteries. It was offering room and board, vegetarian meals, and a trip to Manila, in a neighboring island where the second monastery was located–all expenses paid. This was my sign! They were even giving all participants a monthly allowance so I could get paid a small stipend of $80 a month. Without hesitation, I applied to join and quit the job I didn't want in the first place. It was the first of many things that I manifested freely.

After the monastery retreat, I went on a trip with the same Buddhist organization to Taiwan. I wanted to experience travel as much as I could, but I was concerned about the price. I'd only have to cover the expense of the flight, $400 round trip, so I took the plunge and joined. When I got there, I discovered that the program I was attending, an International Buddhist Youth Conference, was marketed to Ivy League colleges back home in the USA. I felt both completely out of my element and also an insider to the temple ways. Our backend "tour" allowed us to stay before and after conference to volunteer. To my surprise, everyone who attended the conference were given a $500 grant! This more than covered my plane ticket I was so afraid I couldn't afford.

The Buddhist retreats taught me simplicity and deepened my meditation practice. It taught me the reciprocity of the Universe and that the Universe always provides; but also, a behind-the-scenes look at an abundant Buddhist organization built from scratch. My next challenge was to take all the meditation and walking meditation practices. Then I was to apply it to a 500-mile walking journey with a local Filipino that I had met; who called himself a shaman and an expert Filipino martial artist. Together, we walked Palawan island alongside the highway; which was more of a rural road than anything else.

My manifestations grew stronger as I would crave an ice-cold bottle of water after miles and miles of filling our water along local well points that felt questionable. Thankfully, I never got sick, but the hot heat of the sun made the water lukewarm and not the least bit quenching. Local *sari-sari* (variety) stores carried Coca-Cola more than water, which was widely unavailable in the smaller stops. I declared I would get an ice-cold water and after miles of walking we stumbled on a busier town. Obvious by our giveaway travel backpacks, locals usually hosted us every night and let us eat a meal together when we stopped to rest. On that particular day, a local gave us an ice-cold bottle of water. It was the only time that happened and it was exactly what I wanted.

On another day, I was craving an ice-cold beer and I'm not a huge drinker. In fact, all throughout my five years in the toxic relationship, I drank zero alcohol because my ex didn't like it. As you can see, the day I crave beer is a rare bird. On that particular day, my wish was granted. Once again, the only time that we were offered beer throughout the whole walk!

The gap year of living minimalist, on less than $5,000, taught me that little bits of magic were everywhere. I felt *more* support from the Universe when I lived with less.

After my adventures, I launched my freelance business while living in the Manila slums. It was the community my walking partner, (who had now become my boyfriend) had grown up in. My poverty consciousness from ancestral history was running strong. We lived in the shadow of commerce, just a ten-minute walk away from a major mall.

Although many locals live with $2000 a year, I found it hard to adjust to local way of life as a foreigner in my own country. I made about $3,000 my first year of business, but it was the start of feeling perpetually broke. On one occasion, I was having an extra bad day and cried to the Universe for help again. It was the first time I had ever prayed since becoming an Atheist and now slowly finding my way back to God.

"If you're there, God, if you even exist, I need help. I don't have money and I'm asking for some support."

That very same night, a random follower on my Twitter feed decided to gift me $50 out of nowhere. That amount of money goes a long way in the Philippines and lasted me at least a week, which was enough to hold me over until more money arrived. It was the one and only time that happened. I was convinced it was more than just coincidence. My faith strengthened.

Little acts of magic continued to follow me throughout my life and business endeavors. A channel writing session where I called in my next lover, after moving on from the Manila slums. He would be someone I had yet to meet; a traveler, entrepreneur and Filipino who would invite me to Berlin, Germany. That next month, flying back to the Philippines to visit family in Cebu, I met a man through a Cebu Facebook group who fit that exact description and he grew up in Berlin, Germany. Not coincidentally, we were both visiting family in our ancestral homes and realized we were in the same exact village, (in the exact same district or neighborhood) and a three-minute walk around the block—we were literally neighbors! Two weeks into our romance, he invited me to his place in Berlin, which I already knew would happen from the moment we met.

The Second Season: Million Dollar Publishing Business

With the mind-blowing success of my first channel writing session; I did another and asked where I would be in five years. It was 2014 and the answer that came to me was a million-dollar publishing business. For as much truth as my first channel session appeared, I doubted the answer in complete disbelief. By this time, I was still making $20,000 a year at best. The bigness of this answer scared me and intimidated me. I shelved it for later.

The seed was planted. The next year, I rebranded to E-book Queen, but still kept playing small and hiding behind the general graphic, web design, freelance hustle. Fast forward to the summer of 2018. I was pregnant with my baby from my current partner and we had just found out that our baby was measuring small in my womb. They called it SGA (Small Gestational Age) or IUGR (Intra Uterine Growth Restriction). One thing led to another and my chronic high blood pressure landed me in three weeks of hospital bed rest on my 25th week ultrasound. I found myself fighting to keep my baby cooking for as long as she could in my belly.

We toured the NICU, in preparation for the birth of a micro-preemie. I was still in denial that I could magically keep her inside until full term, or at least 34 weeks where premature birth wouldn't be so unknown.

She came at 28 weeks and weighing only 1 lb. 9 oz. The day before her birth, I got a message from her soul when I asked her why she had to be born so early.

"The only way out is through. This is the way to success. This is what I chose for me and you, mama. Money will be taken care of. Don't worry. I'll make it. Share your story. Help women share theirs."

I began to piece it all together. It matched so perfectly with my earlier channel writing message from years ago and the whispers of my soul's calling to start my publishing business felt louder. After my daughter's first birthday, I had a breakthrough moment of inspiration. I knew deep down that self-publishing was part of my path and I had been hiding from my truth; afraid to own it for so long. I grew tired of the monotony of being perpetually "in transition" or "stuck in a rut" and realized that it was my moral obligation to integrate all of me in order to get to my next level. It wasn't about me anymore. It never was. I realized it was about building a life for my daughter and the next generation. Creating a legacy and birthing a new paradigm here on Earth. I decided to create my publishing arm, Dark Quarks Publishing, a nod towards my spiritual awakening path through quantum physics and launched my first multi-author book group experience.

Years of indecision finally collapsed time and within 48 hours, I had my first clients. The book was a first in a series, aptly titled *Birth*, which explores the birthing transformation in business that mothers go through or the rebirthing journey in one's life. It became an international bestselling book on Amazon and paved the way for my *Birth the Book* program.

The birth of this new evolution in my business has birthed a stronger connection to my mission and the legacy that I am here to create. It's about creating a shift in consciousness where masculine ways of dominance are replaced with a more feminine and divine flow. It's about collectively creating a better and more purposeful world where dreams are actualized. Women are the community bearers. Invest in a woman and they give back to the community. Although we still have pay inequality; women have a far bigger sway than one might think. I fully believe this is what the Dalai Lama means when he says, "The world will be saved by the Western Woman".

I fully stand and fully believe in my million-dollar publishing business. What once felt impossible, now feels attainable and inevitable. I am learning to expand, grow, and play a bigger game in my business. I am on track to create my first six figures. I am becoming the leader I was born to be. The teacher, writer and artist that I dreamed of being when I was just a kid. Following my intuition is what lead me, what will always lead me and what will lead me to the expansive vision I am here to create.

Now, more than ever, the world needs more people to stand in their truth, own their stories and build transformative digital businesses that will shift our global economy in support of the greater collective. We are all one. Our own unique genius, our magic, is imperative in this new era. The future is now.

ABOUT JANET BRENT

Janet Brent is an international bestselling author and graphic/web designer, who earned her graphic design degree from the Art Institute of Portland. After designing websites, landing pages, sales funnels, e-books, and print books she decided to combine all her skills and start a self-publishing arm, Dark Quarks Publishing. She now helps women launch solo books and multi-author collaboration books with the bestselling Birth book series and is passionate about helping women own their stories in their business, brand and marketing to impact more people. She is the 'Book Doula' to help you grow your platform. She has been featured in *The Guardian* and is writing her first solo book memoir.

Janet lives in the Pacific Northwest with her partner and is a loving mother to her daughter.

She's avid on Instagram @thejanetbrent and Facebook – https://www.facebook.com/janetbrent/

You can find her work at www.janetbrent.com and more information about the Birth book series at www.birththebook.co

A Life Full of Memories

Millie Kate

Hello, my name is Amelia Kathryn Denhof, although some people call me Millie Kate for short (thanks to my mom who started that). My life as I know it started when I was born at St. Vincent's Hospital in Birmingham, Alabama on August 6 2007 at 11:35 AM.

The woman who gave birth to me is my *"Mom"* also known as, Amelia Blair Hayse. You might be wondering why we both have the same first name (Amelia). That was also my great-great grandmother's name who came over from Italy. Her name was Amelia and so it was passed down in the family. My mom says I was a good baby. My dad's name is, Stanley Gene Denhof. I have one older brother named, Parker Stanley Denhof. Parker was born, June 2 2006 at 5:45 PM. I also have a younger brother, Jackson David Hayse who was born December 5, 2018 at 7:10 PM. When I was a baby, we had a dog named Tucker. We had to get rid of Tucker soon after I was brought home.

I don't remember much, but I do know when I was six months old my dad left me, he was taken away to prison for something he says he didn't do. I was just a baby and honestly do not remember too much about it. I grew up without him in my life or having any contact with him. My mom raised me and my grandparents helped her a lot because she had to work.

Let's skip to when I was three, my mom took us to Disneyworld in Florida! My brother and I had the best time ever. We got to travel on a ferry boat to Disney. I don't really remember all the stuff we did there, but I remember mom letting us get fake tattoos and took us for a ride in a helicopter. At our hotel every morning there were Disney characters dressed up and I was terrified of them. I did NOT want to get my picture taken with them. So, my mom got all their autographs for me in an autograph book. We also attended this really cool movie theater that was in our hotel. It not only felt as if you were in the movie, but it had real cool effects to it for example, as you were riding through water in the movie the theater actually splashed you with water. To this day we still talk about the fun times we had at Disney.

Let's move on to when I was four years old. My brother had just started school! Everyday my grandparents and I would ride their ranger up to their furniture store to drop him off for the bus. We did the same each afternoon when it was time to pick him up from the bus. One day my grandfather (who I call papa) got a call saying someone was at the store waiting for some furniture. He asked if I wanted to come with him and of course, I said "yes!" So, we hopped on the ranger and went up to the furniture store to help the customers that were waiting. That's where I saw the most amazing girl I have ever seen. Her name is Emerson Lee, but everyone called her "Eme." At first, we were really shy towards each other until I went up to her and asked her: "do you want to play tag?" She said yes and we started running around my papa's furniture store playing tag. That was the start of us becoming really good friends!

Let's move on to when I had just turned five years old! It was my first day of school! Like literally. It always seems like the first day of school where I live falls on my actual birthday. I was so excited! I had remembered wanting to go to school so bad when my brother Parker would get on the bus each day headed to school. I remember walking into the classroom and was so shy. The only person I knew was Eme. We all got to pick our seats…which was great! Of course, I chose a seat by Eme and a boy sat next to me named Damien. Later on, throughout Kindergarten, I became very close to my all my classmates. During nap time we would always tell jokes until one of us got in trouble by the teacher. Then we would have to be quiet and actually take our naps. We would always get so excited for lunch or recess. I really miss it. Kindergarten was so much fun.

Let's go on...I had just turned eleven! It was my first day of middle school! It wasn't as exciting, but I still couldn't wait! School was getting harder over the years, but I still had all of my classmates from kindergarten. I loved school and being with my friends. I loved to learn and get to see all the people I had grown up with in school through the years. I was also a part of what we called the "three musketeers." The three musketeers were myself, joined by Eme and Paige. We would always stick together, no matter what. We were nicknamed by the teachers who would call us the three musketeers! The name soon caught on and everyone knew of our little trio by the name. Somehow, in every fight, I was in the middle. I was the one who would be the middle girl and try to bridge things back together between us all. We would always get over our fights pretty quickly though. Our schedule changed so we had different lunch periods that year... which was always the best. Our science teacher at the end of the day would let us take in food and drinks. We all had turns bringing in something for the whole class! Personally, this was my favorite year of school.

Fast forward to now. I am in the eighth grade and am twelve years old. I am now homeschooled. I had to be homeschooled due to something that happened at my school. I am not going into detail about it all because I don't really like talking about it. I always made A's and B's in school, was a great student and a teacher favorite. I'll always miss all of my old friends and I will always

A Life Full of Memories

suffer from it, but that's the position I'm in. I can't wait to start high school for a fresh start with my life because I made a small mistake in middle school that cost me being able to go to school. I have been so sad about it, but there is nothing we can really do about it. The school made some decisions that were unfair and now I must be homeschooled. I am hoping I can go back into public school for high school. It has been my biggest wish. My mom has worked really hard to find a way that I can go back and has even tried to get help so that I can go back to school. I gotta be honest, homeschooling sounded good at the time. I had been begging my mom to homeschool me for a while and so when it was what we had to do I was okay with it at the time. However, now I have no social life, cannot see my friends and am not able to play sports which I loved in school. It gets pretty boring, but that's my story so far! It has had its perks. I got to travel to London and Paris with my mom this year. It was a lot of fun and we got to see a lot of things. My favorite was France. I actually told mom I wouldn't mind living there because it was so pretty and you could walk everywhere. I still miss my friends and I wish I had been able to stay in school. Sometimes it seems like life is really unfair, but as of right now there is no way for me to fix being able to go back to school.

In my spare time now, I love to take photos. I like it so much that I want to become a photographer when I grow up. I also love to edit photos and do a lot of my mom's editing for her photos, Instagram management and video edits for her business. She has inspired me to start my own business. She works hard and she makes money for all of us while working from home. I told her I wanted to do the same thing and work from home. I want to own a photography business with photo editing and graphic design when I get older. I do some now for extra money. I am saving up my money because I want to buy photography equipment and a nice camera so I can take photography classes to learn more about how to do it even better. I got a new dog a couple years ago; her name is Bella. She is so sweet and I love her so much. She goes everywhere I go and she hates for me to be out of her sight. She and I have gotten to be really close. She has been there for me when I have been lonely the past year not going to school anymore. My mom has remarried and even though I give my step-dad a hard time...I really like him. He is fun and I am glad he is around. I want him to be able to adopt me so he can be my dad since I don't have one really.

Sometimes our lives don't turn out the way we think they should. I am still creating my life, but even now there are parts of my life that have turned out different than I would have liked. I am now trying to make my life the best it can be with what I am given and trying to find ways to make it better. I am really glad I have a family that loves me and I know that whatever happens I believe in myself. I have found a real faith and confidence in myself;

that is what keeps me smiling no matter what. My mom has taught me to pray and ask for guidance. I do that and I feel like I am always being taken care of even when I do not see it. It makes me feel peaceful to know I am watched over no matter what.

ABOUT MILLIE KATE

Millie Kate resides with her mom, step-dad and brothers in northeast Mississippi. She loves the outdoors, playing basketball and her dog Bella. She loves to play online with her friends. She is an avid writer, who mainly writes fiction stories. She enjoys watching movies or shows on Netflix. She is addicted to Starbucks and shopping with her mom. She adores horses and hopes to have her own horse one day. Most days you will find her making her own health smoothies in her favorite oversized hoodie.

Millie Kate wants to be a photographer, photo editor and graphic designer when she gets older. She began editing photos on her Instagram account a year ago and has built her Instagram account over time.

She edits photos for her mom's business and helps her mother manage her social media. She recently was hired on as Social Media Manager with Blair Hayse International, LLC. With the new position she has taken on editing videos and helping with a new virtual television project.

Millie Kate does freelance editing and graphic design for extra money (she is saving for photography equipment).

You can follow her on Instagram: @jupiter.royale

If you are interested in hiring her for freelance projects or want to get quotes you can email her at: lia.kathryn@yahoo.com

Go Ahead and Jump

Eleni ELNRG

"Eleni! Can I get another Miller Lite and four Vegas bombs?"

The sounds of clashing bottles, laughter and country music flowing out of the jukebox made it difficult to hear.

"I'm sorry what was that?" I ask.

The young man repeats himself. I grab his requests and continue along my usual routine of sprinting back and forth, dancing around, telling jokes and slinging drinks. I had bartended on and off for portions of my adult life. This place was by far my favorite. The local honky tonk, generation after generation, had been served in this local gem. Where the dust was as old as the long-outdated blinds, peanuts were served and their shells tossed on the floor. A happy place where fights were seldom and good people from all walks of life gathered. As a single mom, it was the perfect fit. I would get to spend days with my daughter and work only a few nights to be able to provide.

I really didn't have to sacrifice much time with her and I still got to have fun! I loved the conversations, the music and definitely the ca$h.

However, things began to shift for me when my daughter started attending school. I was now getting less time with her. On the weekends, I typically worked at night and was tired during the day. She was not getting the best of me. Instead, she was just getting the *rest* of me. I started noticing a change in her behavior. She was acting out in school. She was missing me and expressing it in the only way she knew how. I began to feel the ending of this life phase as it started to unfold. It made sense. The alignment was definitely sliding. In August, I was co-author in a book that was widely successful and offered opportunities to revisit my former corporate passion; public speaking. Yes! I could see the opportunities starting to develop and my vision was much larger than this small rural town. I knew there was more to come, but my reality at that time had me feeling very bound. It was a huge leap of faith leaving a comfortable lifestyle and becoming a single mom. Nonetheless, it was necessary in order to provide my daughter and myself with a healthy supportive situation. Working in the bar our needs were met, but there was not much energy left for me to pursue my calling. I was uncertain how to transition into the new and still be able to financially care for my daughter. In my heart I knew it would be soon. It had to be. My ever-present gratitude and love for all parts of my life were beginning to get tainted with spritzes of fear or resentment at what was my daily existence.

I faced the uncertainty with the only way I knew how to truly seek an answer. I hit my knees in prayer. I humbly expressed my gratitude for all of the wonderful people I had met because of my present work, the fundraising we were able to accomplish for the women's shelter I volunteered at and the financial stability it provided for my daughter and me.

I simply asked...

"Lord, is there a lesson I am meant to learn? So many amazing situations are lining up, why am I still bartending?"

Clear as a bell I heard these words.

"Divine Love."

I reflected on that deep within my heart, felt a sure confidence the meaning would soon present itself and present itself it did! My next shift, I was working solo and it was a packed house. I'm talking...standing room only. I was literally doing cardio to keep up. I was in my zone. In the midst of the madness I encountered a belligerent woman. She proceeded to cuss me up and down. For no other reason than her tequila must have hit her Ferrari fast. In that moment I didn't want to yell, toss her out or quite frankly have any type of confrontation. I heard the answer to the prayer I had asked. Divine Love. Suddenly,

I saw that woman with empathy. I thought about my own life being a recovered alcoholic and how many scenes I had made in my drinking days. Perhaps, this woman was just like me. Perhaps, she would wake up tomorrow digesting that same guilt, shame and remorse my alcoholism always served up for me. Facing myself in the mirror the next day was always worse than the actual physical hangover. I felt sorrow for that woman. I felt compassion for her. I prayed for her. From that second on, I knew exactly what God's message was to me: loving tolerance for all. I became very mindful of gossip and how I interacted with people. I simply became more deliberate with my thoughts when it came to how I viewed others. We are all just people, aren't we? Some of us have more difficult lessons to learn than others and what business is it of mine to pass judgment on it.

Well, it didn't take long of putting this into action that the universe delivered in a big way! I had a passion project I had been collaborating on for a few months with one of my best friends. He was absolutely divinely sent to help me execute this idea. His area of expertise could give this project life. I boldly shared this vision with a spiritual mentor and guess what? He loved the idea and decided to invest in me. Investing enough that I could leave bartending and fearlessly focus on my project. I cannot fully express the gratitude I felt in my heart. I was elated. Buzzing with possibility. Motivated in a way I had never been. I felt renewed. Empowered. Validated. Supported. I was invigorated and ready to leap. That weekend I turned in my two weeks resignation letter.

Two weeks came and went quickly. I felt the love of my community as they wished me off. My dreams were awake and I was ready to get to work. There was a problem, I was not getting replies from my investor. Text after text. Email after email. With each hit of the send button my heart sank a little more. I kept hope that something must have come up. He was an extremely successful man. I was certain my situation was not the most pressing project for him at the time. Being knowledgeable about law of attraction I was very aware of the damage fear-based thinking would cause in this situation. I utilized my time enjoying the holidays with my girl. Feeling true joy. Finding so many humbled blessings. I began to pay greater attention to meditation and fine tuning my process. I studied philosophers and spiritual leaders. I took time to nourish my mind and my soul. I did my best to keep a loving outlook. Once again, I consulted my source.

"Lord, I know you have not led me away from being able to provide for my daughter to go down a dark road. Show me what I am supposed to learn."

The next day I received a message on social media from a woman I had went to high school with. Though we didn't connect often, I absolutely considered her a friend. She was someone I would randomly cross paths with during different times in my life. As a mother, her message was devastating to me. Her son was in a terrible accident and at a local trauma center in a coma. She was aware I did healing work and was willing to pay me to come work with him. Despite my situation, I had never before taken a dime to heal and I wasn't about to start. I knew it would be beneficial not only to the young man and his family, but it would also give me a sense of purpose through service. Without hesitation I told her I would be there the following day. The next morning, in preparation for going to do the healing session on Tyler, I prayed and meditated. I asked for God to work through me and help me be of service. Again, clear as can be, I heard the words:

"You are not the healer; you are the coach."

I knew exactly what this meant. One of the lecturers I had been following, Dr. Joe Dispenza, focused much of his research on the body's ability to heal and repair itself. A light bulb went off! I have complete access to this young man's subconscious mind. I would use the philosophies I had learned and fuel it with energy work. I could hardly wait to arrive and try this out. I went into the room with upbeat hopeful energy and could feel right away that he was going to recover from this. I spoke to him as his future healed self and we went through the session. Within hours his lungs began to function again. I felt such love and fullness in my heart. I was so blessed to be a part of this miraculous journey. My energy shifted from worry about my investor and decision to leap...to motivation in helping Tyler. I went to work with him a couple of times a week and within three weeks he was awake. I kept working with his mindset and brain function. He was quickly surpassing the expectations of doctors and crushing obstacles. Day by day more "divine downloads" were given to me to help Tyler and expand the potential of this project. In one of them, I was instructed to find Dr. Joe Dispenza's email and ask for additional guidance. So, I did, and he replied! He took an interest in Tyler's case and not only offered valuable advice, but to work with him at one of his seminars! This was another situation in which following divine guidance brought me immense joy. Little by little, any financial fears I was having were squelched. Miracles happened and all my needs were met. Earth angels stepped up, I had the support and encouragement of friends, my soul sister and my two brothers. Everyone kept guiding me to stay on my path.

Once Tyler was moved to his rehab facility, I started going only once a week. I asked God, what I was to do next? Where was this path leading me? This is when the mother of all "divine downloads came to me. It was a complete blue print of how to duplicate this process and teach people all over the world how to heal their bodies. I went to work immediately. It led to laying out the foundation work for ELNRG Healing Coaching. Everything was shown to me from the intake process all the way to execution of the healing sessions. I was shown how to grow this from a seed to an international company. I was guided who to ask to mentor me and where to find the funding. Every bit of it has lined up.

I feel called to share this journey with you, because it represents the truth. Faith is lack of fear. Once you find your soul's calling and you come to understand that you truly are divinely supported in every way; there is absolutely nothing to fear. Today, I could not be more thankful for the initial investment delay. If that had panned out as promised, I would not have been afforded the time to focus on Tyler and receive this guidance from above. The high of the soul I felt as each download resulted in more and more spectacular outcomes. This beautiful plan my higher power has laid out for me. A mission that will help the masses. I feel like I have found my jackpot. In the meantime, everything is always working out for me. Bills are paid, food is on the table and an endless supply of support. I have found enormous value in my friends, my family and my spiritual practice.

If you are feeling unhappy in your life circumstance. Trust. That is your spirit telling you that you are out of alignment. Take the chance and pursue with full trust to go find your calling. Happiness is the intention of life.

Van Halen said it best… "Might as well JUMP! Go ahead and jump!"

Do it! Your purpose is waiting for you.

ABOUT ELENI ELNRG

Eleni Yiambilis, founder of ELNRG.com is a motivational public speaker, certified Life and Thought Process Coach and developer of ELNRG Healing Coaching System. She has found her calling and passion in empowering individuals to shatter self-limiting beliefs and behaviors. Through ELNRG she helps people retrain the brain in process of thought; using her system appropriately named "The Gratitude Adjustment" as well as recover from illness and injury by opening people up to the capabilities of the human body. Eleni has spoken across the United States as an advocate for nutrition and fitness as a Health and Wellness Advisor for the Rastelli Foods Group. It is her belief that by eliminating toxins from our diets and honoring our bodies through fitness, it is possible to achieve a higher vibrational frequency and in turn attract and manifests one's desires and abundance more efficiently. Today she continues to speak internationally, helping people see the full potential in who they are both mentally and physically.

A survivor of a difficult road tainted by multiple forms of addiction, childhood abuse and domestic violence; Eleni has learned to take painful life situations, apply gratitude and service to identify the blessings thus facilitating the growth for forgiveness. Through fine tuning the thought process from fear-based to faith-based, she has developed programs to assist others to achieve the same freedom. With over 10 years' experience as a Reiki Practitioner and crystal healer; she believes and teaches others how to attract their most vibrant fulfilling life.

Eleni resides in southern New Jersey and is blessed with a spectacular daughter. She is a dedicated volunteer at a local women's and children shelter where she responds to calls, comforts and counsels domestic violence assault victims. She also offers Reiki and life coaching to victims. Additionally, she assists the shelter in fundraising efforts. As a well-known trainer in her area, Eleni has a true passion for fitness and enjoys utilizing the outdoors to help others feel healthy or inspired. Creative by nature, she enjoys upcycling antiques, woodworking and any artistic venture. Her favorite place to be is by any natural body of water or cuddled up with her daughter.

Find her on the web at www.Elnrg.com

Facebook - Elnrg

Join her healing empowerment group
The ELNRG Collective Healing Circle
on Facebook for additional support.

Nice Girls Don't Get the Plush Corner Office *(Or Do They?)*

Blair Hayse

A lot can be said about corporate America and even more can be said about the woman who has risen to the top of the ladder in it. Because the hike up the corporate ladder is one of long hours, underpaid work, massive deadlines and sacrifices most people are not willing to make. It doesn't happen overnight (well, maybe if you choose to sleep with the boss), but in the normal hike up it comes with a lot of time and consistency. It comes with them seeing you are loyal to your job and the company over everything else. It comes with being able to handle your own. It comes with being able to fire someone or even worse, testify to put someone in jail (yes, I had to do that). It comes with rising to the top on every occasion. It comes with working insane hours and not being able to be at all your kid's school functions. It comes with going into work sick because as the CEO you cannot just "call out". It comes with long hours and lots of coffee to meet hundreds of deadlines on reports that if you ask me, are all the same things written a hundred different ways. It comes with analyzing numbers and knowing what needs to shift. It comes with being aware of payroll, labor, purchases, revenue and the list goes on. It comes with knowing who works under you and their strengths (and their weaknesses for that matter). It comes with being on call 24/7 and literally never getting a "day off". It comes with choosing to deal with disasters of any kind. It comes with being decisive in a split second. It comes with being hard on yourself and those that work for you; because you expect the best. It comes with your eyes hurting because you worked on a budget for umpteen hours and now all you see when you close your eyes are graphs with numbers. It comes with being so overloaded that you do not answer texts or phone calls until days later and sometimes never at all. Family and friends learn that you are usually unreachable. Some understood because they knew of the job demands. Others, took it personally and would create more drama around the fact you didn't answer a text or call in the appropriate time they thought you should. I could go on and on. This is literally just a sliver of what rising to the top of a corporate career takes.

However, if you are woman, this climb is even more difficult. You are pushed to prove yourself. You are underestimated. You usually have to fight for the salary you deserve. You have to deal with extra pressures and lots of sexual comments (emphasize *LOTS*). The one thing that you deal with more than any man in a corporate CEO chair... are the mean girls. You know...the ones who hate you just because you are the CEO. They hate you because you made it to the top. They hate you because you outshine them. This is the most unfortunate part of a woman making it in the corporate world. Women can get jealous and not even know how her jealousy is justified. They spread rumors about you. They work against you with your team dividing your team morale. They create problems just to see you sweat. It is craziness. When I hear talk about women empowering women, I chuckle. Have they ever lived in the corporate chair at the top? Obviously not. The worst kind of woman is not the one who takes the knife and stabs you in the back. Why? Because you *KNOW* she is your enemy. You are already looking out for her. You already know she is contemplating your fall. No, it is the one who tries to befriend you just to slash you down. It is the one who betrays your confidence because you thought you could trust her. It is the enemy disguised as someone you do not see ever doing this, then you are blind sighted by the hit. Trust me, being blind-sighted is my biggest pet-peeve.

These are the reasons you hear the term "nice girls don't get the corner office". It is true. You need tough boundaries (and really tough skin) to sit in the corner office. Is it lonely at the top? Heck yeah it is. It is lonely because you are there and *they* are not. I know the feeling all too well. It means eating your salad in a hurry at your desk while others go off to eat lunch in groups. It means declining drinks after work because friendship and work do NOT mix. You are a leader and you have to separate yourself to be one. It is hard and it is pressuring. It will cause days you cry and days you wonder if it is worth it. There are days you wonder if punching a time card and just making minimum wage is actually worth consideration. You will feel like you are going crazy. You will question everyone around you. You will learn to not trust easily or ever. You will learn that boundaries are necessary. You will learn that the feeling of success and prestige comes with a costly price tag.

This my friend, is the reason women who rise to the top are to be commended. They are to be applauded. They are to be given extra credit. I can also guarantee this is why only a small percentage of women are millionaires or and even smaller percentage are billionaires. Over half of the already small percentage of millionaires and billionaires inherited their wealth. This leaves an even smaller percentage to be self-made wealth. Yes, because this road is not one many can survive. It is not one that many can handle. So, for those who rise to the top...for those who choose to break that glass ceiling and bust through it with power...cheers girlfriend. I will gladly tip my flute of champagne your way and tell you I am freaking proud of you. You achieved something a lot of women cannot do emotionally, physically or mentally. I am loving you and telling you that I understand what you went through to get there...because I am her. If no one has told you they are proud of you...I am saying it to you now. I am so proud of you!!

What I put above, is not just me analyzing the woman CEO, but it is me sharing what I know because I lived it. I breathed it. I was her. I sat in the big plush corner office that comes with a lot of backstabbing, rumors and loneliness. I remember thinking there must be a different way to do this. There must be a way to provide as a single mom with two children and no support from the father. There must be a way to have success without the costly price tag. Without the sacrifices. Without the hurt. Without being lonely at the top. These are many of the reasons (add in there a 4-hour daily commute) that I chose to look at opening my own business. I was exhausted and I mean literally on ALL levels. My dad, who I admire more than anyone I know, tried for years to get me to open my own consulting business. He saw in me what I thought I only could achieve in the CEO chair. Is it not crazy, how we think we know it all in our younger days? I thought he was as stupid as they come. In reality, he had lived the corporate life and his loyalty of 30+ years was dashed in a day when they forced him to early retirement because of "restructure". I ignored his pleas and kept traveling the path of corporate conditioning that status is to achieve in that corner office. Come to think of it, I ignored a lot of my dad's advice through the years, only to wish I had listened to it sooner. Am I alone in this?

The day I chose to start consulting independently, I hired a firm to represent me and book me. They would send the proposals to me where I could review them and either accept or decline the job. I thought this was a move in a better direction. Once again, pushing aside the fact I needed to go all in and just start my own business. It ended up being a lot of sacrifices, especially being on the road for weeks without seeing my children. I thought maybe I needed a career change, but honestly this is all I knew. I had worked hard to become an expert in my field. I never lacked for opportunities and my inbox stayed full of competitors offering enticing packages to hire me. I was in demand. Why would I change careers? As a business woman, It just did not make sense. Instead, I took the plunge and started my own business on the side while still in my corporate job. Remember where I talked about long hours? Now, take that and add a side business into the mix. I would take client calls in my car on my lunch break. I struggled to make my business work. I still had the comfort of a salary and the urgency for my side business to work was clearly not there.

Then, I lost my job. Without any warning, it was gone. It was five days before Christmas. I remember thinking I needed to deal with the emotional blow, but in my industry, there is a lot of shifting and it is common to change jobs quickly. I took my time to get through Christmas and started to focus on my business. I had clients, but I struggled to bring in the income I would need to replace my salary. I just could not get it to work the way I thought it should. Something was not clicking. I had hired a successful coach and I had done everything she told me to do, but nothing. I decided to go back into the corporate chair and once again bargained with myself that I would work this business while doing my job with financial security. Want to guess if that happened? Eh, yeah, you know the answer. I was too comfortable with misery. I wish current me could go kick past me in the ass sometimes. Literally. I was so stubborn. Two days into my new job I was not feeling good and my best friend persuaded me to take a pregnancy test. It was positive. I was in disbelief. We were not trying. I was not ready for another child in my new relationship. I dealt with overwhelming emotions, exhaustion and nausea for months. My depression went off the scales and I couldn't deal with my job pressures. Especially with no medication for anxiety and depression. Plus, the hormones. I was a hot mess. In ALL essence of the words *HOT MESS*. On top of that I was having relationship issues due to my in-laws who were trying to divide my partner and I. I remember getting to work and being so exhausted. I would cry in my office when no one was looking. I remember wondering why everything was landing on my shoulders at one time. Why was work so overwhelming? Why was my pregnancy so difficult this time? Why were my in-laws hating me and trying to break up my relationship? I worked through the pregnancy and when I say worked...I mean actually, physically, worked hard. We were in the middle of opening a hotel. Working insane long hours. Moving furniture. Doing heavy work both mental and physical. No surprise, I was admitted to the hospital early to have the baby. When he arrived, he was rushed to NICU before I could even hold him because he couldn't breathe. I was frightened. His lungs were under developed and we were in NICU for a week. The next few months were a lot of hospital visits, a battle with RSV on his already weak lungs and a lot of serious allergy issues causing colic. We were battling it all on no sleep and work was the last thing on my mind. Guess what? Work still contacted me at all hours, yet refused to pay me for my maternity leave. I had to fight to get just a fraction of what I was owed. I realized then, my dad was right. Companies do not care about YOU. They care about their business. I was at a cross roads. Same road of comfort or take a new path. New path won.

I took the plunge into my business and what happened over the next few months was not your overnight success story. Matter of fact, it was a downright nightmare. We were forced out of our home with 30 days' notice because of a bad roof the landlord refused to fix. I had a small baby whose health was fragile. We had no idea where we would go. We started looking for a new home and packing boxes. We moved and it left us financially strained. I was struggling to show up in my business, dealing with some crazy hormones still and stressed with money. We made all the extra money we could. We sold things and did odd jobs. My fiancé worked hard, but his paychecks couldn't replace my salary we were used to getting. We fell behind further and further. The more we fell behind the more I found myself stricken with panic attacks and stress. Things spiraled out of financial control. I had no idea how we were going to pay all our bills and something had to be sacrificed. Two generous job offers came my way without me even looking for them. I tried to imagine that this was sign from above of answered prayer, but I knew in my gut I would regret it. I knew if I took them, I would end up at this crossroads again. I declined. Then, the day came I lost my car. We literally had no way to get around, was stressed on bills and was a month away from losing our place to live. We had just experienced a death in our immediate family and I had no idea how I was going to get to the funeral except rely on family members to give us a ride. I remember crying. Then, I chose to wipe my tears away. Adjust my focus and say to myself...I am going to do this. I quit playing small. I quit doubting my abilities in the online space. I quit over thinking if I was doing things the way a coach told me to do them. I brought my 19 years of corporate experience to the table and went all in. I mean *ALL IN!* I had nothing to lose at this point. It was up to me to make this choice or go back to that plush corner office

I had grown to loathe. I did not want to go back there! Within a month my business exploded. It grew to nearly half of my monthly corporate salary. In two months over half. In three months, I made more than I ever made in that lonely corner office! WHAT!!?? In one day, I made a $20k sale. Business took off and as it escalated bigger, I fell even more in love with my new business. Then, the other shoe fell...

I found out that in the same way the corner office was lonely, there were still women who would try to sabotage my career. I found out jealousy was still alive online the same as it was offline. I found out things still took a lot of effort, hours and consistency. It all still took a lot of drive and being able to be thick skinned. All the things I thought I was going to escape from the corporate office was right here in the online one too. I then realized that escaping all those things was not what I needed. I needed to learn how to manage them. I needed to learn how to rise above this and use it to create something of value. I needed to stop running. I needed to figure out how to deal with these issues head on. I realized; it had to do with energy. It had to do with the same hurt and anger we hold when someone steals our program idea or tries to sabotage our career. These can be the emotions that either make or break us. We can view them as negative emotions; or we can change the energy into positive forces that propel us into steps of action. The very steps that show us the way to the top. We can learn how to be cautious and not blend business too deeply into other areas. We can learn the multi-million-dollar CEO *NEEDS* boundaries. It takes being aware of those you allow into your inner circle of trust. It takes a *LOT* of work. Nothing of real value is going to happen overnight. It is not going to come without major action. You might not can get rid of the workplace bullies or the occasional stab in the back, but you can choose your attitude towards it. You can choose to love and with that love comes fierce boundaries because you love yourself even more. You can choose to take the negative emotions and transmute that energy into positive actions of power to fuel your dreams. You can have the freedom and flexibility of working from home in an office (maybe not as nice as the corporate one you left), but happy and loved. Why? Because you are allowing yourself to be the nice girl (with boundaries of course) with the fancy CEO title AND your family around you AND your cup of coffee AND your laptop, all the while, the mean girls that fuel your passion are just faintly heard. You find a tribe that will adjust their shades so that you do not have to dull your shine. That will boost you to reach your next goals. That will encourage you to hire that attorney to protect your intellectual property when a client steals it and will be there to cheer you on when you have a major success in your business. You can sit back and sip tea (or wine – no judgement from me) and be grateful for the journey that got you where you are today.

You just proved *NICE* girls can have the plush corner office.

May this remind you...you are magic my dear friend.

Just as it reminds me daily...that I am magic too.

Yes, I am highly sure of it.

Cheers my boss babe!

Enjoy it *ALL* because you can and deserve it *ALL!*

ABOUT BLAIR HAYSE

Blair was born and raised in Tupelo, Mississippi. After graduating high school in 1999 she lived in Birmingham and Florence, Alabama before moving back to Itawamba County, Mississippi in 2008. She is an avid yoga lover, free spirit, shopping addict and mom to three beautiful children Parker, Millie and Jackson. She is currently residing in Northeast Mississippi with her husband Jeremy and enjoys traveling in her spare time.

Blair has a 19-year background in Corporate America where she worked with billion-dollar companies such has Hilton, Marriott, IHG, Starwood and others. She was called in to create a massive profit in a business so that the company could flip the business or make an investment.

She specialized in working with business investments that had gone bad so that a quick profit could be achieved. Some of her projects included businesses that had been costing the company money for five years straight and she brought them to a massive profit level in just six months. This became her signature method of seven figures in six months that she used over and over.

Blair created a legacy in the corporate world where she was sought out for her expertise. The corporate life while exciting and well-paying was exhausting to the single mom of two kids. Blair brought her skills to the online world where she now helps online businesses create a massive flow of profit in a short amount of time. This allowed her the freedom to enjoy her life, travel more and give time to her family.

Blair owns and publishes a digital magazine for entrepreneurs: *Seven Figure Online CEO*. You can locate the magazine through Facebook @sevenfigureonlineceo and they always welcome new online entrepreneurs into their circle. Blair currently owns Blair Hayse Publishing which publishes books including the collaboration project 'She is Magic' series. Blair is soon launching a collaboration TV series, BE – Empowerment TV, with Eleni ELNRG.

Blair currently is a Massive Profit Growth Strategist Coach, two-time best-selling author and international speaker. She has founded a Facebook group, "Seven Figures in Six Months" for those who are ready to scale their businesses to six and seven figures. She also offers free resources including her Your Way to $100k Workshop, a 30 Days to 10k Course, her signature program Seven Figure Society, an annual conference and private coaching to her clients.

To connect with Blair:
www.blairhayse.com
Facebook: @blairhayse
Instagram: @blairhayse

Would you like to publish your story in a collaboration piece?

We are now putting together...
She is Magic Too...

Spots are now open for you to join us and share your story of magic with the world.

Please connect with us through the link below for more information:

https://blairhayse.kartra.com/page/blairhaysepublishing

Made in the USA
Middletown, DE
14 April 2020

89353026R00119